Assessing Evaluation Studies

The Case of

BILINGUAL EDUCATION STRATEGIES

Michael M. Meyer and
Stephen E. Fienberg, Editors

Panel to Review Evaluation Studies of Bilingual Education
Committee on National Statistics
Commission on Behavioral and Social Sciences and Education
National Research Council

NATIONAL ACADEMY PRESS
Washington, D.C. 1992

This project was supported by funds from the U.S. Department of Education.

Library of Congress Catalog Card No. 92-64011
International Standard Book Number 0-309-04728-5

Additional Copies of this report are available from:

National Academy Press
2101 Consitution Avenue N.W.
Washington, D.C. 20418

S621

Printed in the United States of America

Panel to Review Evaluation Studies of Bilingual Education

STEPHEN E. FIENBERG *(Chair)*, Department of Mathematics and Statistics and Osgoode Hall Law School, York University

BARBARA F. FREED, College of Humanities and Social Sciences, Carnegie Mellon University

KENJI HAKUTA, School of Education, Stanford University

LYLE V. JONES, Department of Psychology, University of North Carolina

KATHRYN B. LASKEY, School of Information Technology and Engineering, George Mason University

LUIS C. MOLL, School of Education, University of Arizona

P. DAVID PEARSON, College of Education, University of Illinois

JOHN E. ROLPH, The RAND Corporation, Santa Monica, California

PAUL R. ROSENBAUM, Department of Statistics, The Wharton School, University of Pennsylvania

DONALD B. RUBIN, Department of Statistics, Harvard University

KEITH F. RUST, Westat, Inc., Rockville, Maryland

BURTON H. SINGER, Department of Epidemiology and Public Health, Yale University

HERBERT L SMITH, Population Studies Center, University of Pennsylvania

MICHAEL M. MEYER, *Study Director* (Carnegie Mellon University)

MICHELE L. CONRAD, *Senior Project Assistant*

Contents

Preface

In October of 1990 the United States Department of Education requested the National Research Council to convene a panel to review two major evaluation studies of bilingual education. The panel was formed in early 1991 and given the following charge:

> The Panel to Review Evaluation Studies of Bilingual Education will review and assess the methodology of data collection and analysis of two major studies to evaluate bilingual education programs: a national longitudinal study of the effectiveness of instruction of limited-English-proficient students and a study to compare the effectiveness of three different instructional strategies for bilingual education for such students. The three strategies are immersion (teachers understand Spanish, but respond in English), early exit (students are placed in classes conducted in English as soon as possible), and late exit (both languages are maintained and a proficiency in English is developed over time).
>
> In the first phase of its study, the panel will:
>
> 1. review the methods of data collection and analysis for potential sources of error and assess implications for some of the principal findings;
> 2. assess whether additional analyses of the data from either study would strengthen or broaden the findings and, if so, recommend some analyses that could be carried out; and
> 3. suggest alternative ways to compare the different instructional strategies and provide advice to the Department of Education Planning and Evaluation Service on commissioning and managing similar evaluation studies in the future.

If, in the panel's assessment, additional data analyses are warranted, and if the Department of Education and the panel agree, the panel would, in the second phase of its study, commission and review the analyses.

The two studies reviewed are *The National Longitudinal Study of the Evaluation of the Effectiveness of Services for Language-Minority Limited-English-Proficient Students* and *The Longitudinal Study of Immersion Strategy, Early-exit and Late-exit Transitional Bilingual Education Programs for Language-Minority Children.* Throughout the report the panel has adopted the words Longitudinal Study to describe the first study and Immersion Study to describe the second study. These terms are misleading, but they were the language that the Department of Education adopted in its description of the studies. For the record, the panel notes that both of the studies are longitudinal and that the "immersion" study does not have a real immersion component.

The panel's conclusions and recommendations are presented in Chapter 6. This is a very short chapter and readers who have a limited amount of time may wish to turn there first.

The panel first met in March of 1991, shortly after the final report for the Immersion Study was made available. Subsequent meetings were held in June and December of 1991. This report is the result of the panel's deliberations.

At the outset we thank the panel for its dedication to this project and its willingness to work in a very short time frame.

Many people made generous contributions to the work of the panel. We thank the many staff members of the U.S. Department of Education who attended our meetings, answered our innumerable questions, and provided mountains of reports, interim reports and background material. In particular, the efforts of James English and David Moguel were invaluable. The contractors for the two studies, Development Associates and Research Triangle Institute for the Longitudinal Study and Aguirre International for the Immersion Study, attended our first meeting, provided us with background materials and responded to many questions. Graham Burkheimer of Research Triangle Institute, Malcolm Young of Development Associates, and David Ramirez of Aguirre International were especially helpful. Wallace Lambert of McGill University shared with the panel his experiences in the Canadian immersion studies; his discussions helped to set the stage for many of our own deliberations.

The Departments of Statistics and of Academic Computing and Media at Carnegie Mellon University provided release time to allow Michael Meyer to direct the study and also provided excellent computing support.

Miron Straf, director of Committee on National Statistics, was always available to answer our questions and to assist us through the operations of the National Research Council.

The Committee on National Statistics provided valuable input into the report, and in particular encouraged us to expand the scope of our comments to the general domain of educational research.

PREFACE ix

Finally, we would like to thank the staff of the Committee on National Statistics, especially our senior project assistant, Michele Conrad. Michele kept the panel informed, organized meetings, provided editorial assistance, suffered our changing schedules, and still managed to keep a cheery disposition. The report would have taken a lot longer to complete without her assistance.

Stephen E. Fienberg, *Chair*
Michael M. Meyer, *Study Director*
Panel to Review Evaluation Studies
of Bilingual Education

1

Bilingual Education in the United States

This report can be read on at least two different levels. On a broad level, the report can be viewed as a discussion of statistical methods approriate for education, particularly bilingual education studies, using two specific studies as case examples. On a more narrow level, the report discusses specific details of two U.S. Department of Education studies about bilingual education. (The report does not explicitly consider organization issues; for these we refer the reader to Atkinson and Jackson (1992)).

This chapter provides the context for the studies under review, some initial words about assessment of studies, and an overview of the report.

RESEARCH CONTEXT

The research reviewed in this report exists in the context of a broad and rich array of research traditions on bilingualism and bilingual education. From an academic perspective, the hybrid fields of psycholinguistics, sociolinguistics, and education have viewed bilingualism both as a topic intrinsically worthy of investigation and as a phenomenon that offers interesting perspectives on, or even critical tests of, theories about linguistic, cognitive, and social processes. These theoretical views of bilingualism—such as the cognitive effects of bilingualism, the social correlates of knowing two or more languages, the nature of the relationship among languages, and the relationship between language and its family, school, community and societal contexts—provide a background for understanding of bilingual education practice and policy; these issues are discussed in Fishman (1977) and Hakuta (1986).

From an applied perspective, bilingual education has generated research under two distinct sociological conditions: one in which the students are native speakers of the predominant language of the society and the other in which they are immigrants or are members of minority-language groups. For example, Canadian bilingual education programs are noted for their success in promoting the learning of French by English speakers through a method called "immersion," in which English monolingual children begin their schooling experience exclusively in French, with the gradual phasing in of instruction in the native language. A wealth of research shows two key results: these students learn French at levels far beyond what they would have achieved in traditional French language instruction programs, and these students perform in English at a level comparable to their peers who are in monolingual English instruction. This situation has been characterized as "additive bilingualism" (Lambert, 1980), in which the second language is added without detriment to the native language. Useful overviews of the Canadian research are Lambert (1992) and Swain (1992) and the references contained in those articles.

In contrast to the Canadian context, bilingual education in the United States exists primarily as a means to aid the transition of immigrant and linguistic minority children into English. Program evaluations seek information on the efficiency by which English is taught, with little or no interest in maintenance of the native language. The situation in which the native language of immigrants and minorities has low social prestige value has been called "subtractive bilingualism." It typically results in monolingualism in the majority language within two to three generations. The United States has been home to speakers of practically every modern language, yet these linguistic resources have not been captured, and Americans have a well-deserved reputation as incompetent in foreign languages.

Linguistic issues in education—both in additive and subtractive bilingual settings—are of increasing importance in this era of global interdependence and cross-national mobility of workers in all industrialized nations. The Canadian research effort in bilingual education in an additive setting has been exemplary for its blend of theory, empirical tests, and sustained effort. The evaluation efforts in the United States—the subject of this report—provide an important barometer not just of the effectiveness of bilingual education, but perhaps more importantly of U.S. research capacity and policy in this area.

POLICY CONTEXT

President Johnson signed the Bilingual Education act as Title VII of the Elementary and Secondary Education Act (ESEA) on January 2, 1968. The act was reauthorized in 1974, 1978, 1984 and 1988, and it is scheduled for reauthorization in 1992. This section offers a brief sketch of the bilingual education policy context from 1968 to the late 1980s, when the the studies reviewed in this report were completed, with primary focus on the early 1980s, when the requests for proposals for these studies were developed.

Probably the most important issue in understanding the context of bilingual education is the specification of the role of the native languages of students. The original legislation provided for the training of teachers and aides to work with students with limited English skills, as well as for the development of materials and activities to involve parents in the schools. It was limited to students from poor backgrounds and did not prescribe use of the native language or culture in instruction. By 1974 the act was expanded to include students regardless of poverty, and more importantly, it required inclusion of the child's native language and culture "to the extent necessary to allow a child to progress effectively through the educational system" (quoted in Crawford, 1989).

Fueling the issue of native language use was the *Lau* v. *Nichols* decision by the Supreme Court (414 U.S. 563, 1974) and its interpretation by the Office for Civil Rights (OCR) in the Office of Education. The court decision was based on Title VI of the Civil Rights Act and ruled that students with limited English proficiency, in the absence of treatment, were "effectively foreclosed from any meaningful education." The court eschewed specific remedies, noting: "Teaching English to the students of Chinese ancestry who do not speak the language is one choice. Giving instructions to this group in Chinese is another. There may be others."

The OCR response, officially titled *Task-Force Findings Specifying Remedies Available for Eliminating Past Educational Practices Ruled Unlawful under Lau v. Nichols*, was issued on August 11, 1975. The remedies went beyond the *Lau* decision: they required that bilingual education of some form be provided at the elementary school level in cases where injustice was found; an English as a Second Language (ESL) program was deemed acceptable at the middle school level. Although the remedies did not have the status of federal regulations, they were effectively used as such in disputes with school districts.

On the legislative front, questions were raised about the effectiveness of bilingual education programs as early as the late 1970s. One study, conducted by the American Institutes for Research (AIR) under contract from the Office of Planning, Budget and Evaluation (OPBE) (Dannoff, 1978), compared students in 38 ESEA Title VII programs with those students in ESL classes; it failed to find positive impact. However, it did find evidence for students' being kept in bilingual programs even after they had attained proficiency in English and a sizable proportion of program personnel who supported a philosophy of maintenance bilingualism. The AIR study had many shortcomings. However, the panel wishes to emphasize that *the failure to find effects in poorly designed evaluative studies should not be taken as evidence that such effects do not exist.*

The 1978 reauthorization of the Bilingual Education Act required that the programs it supported involve the use of the native language and was quite directive in requesting research on a variety of questions. Section 742 of the act instructed the Assistant Secretary of Education to "coordinate research activities of the National Institute of Education (NIE) with the Office of Bilingual Education (OBE), the National Center for Education Statistics (NCES) and other appropriate agencies in order to develop a national research program for bilingual education."

As a result, in the spring of 1978, an Education Division Coordinating Committee was established to implement the broad mandate. This committee came to be called the "Part C Committee," named after the part of the legislation requiring its establishment. The committee was chaired by the Deputy Assistant Secretary for Education (Policy Development) and included representatives from the National Institute of Education, the National Center for Education Statistics, the Office of Bilingual Education (later the Office of Bilingual Education and Minority Language Affairs (OBEMLA)) and the Office of Evaluation and Dissemination (later the Office of Planning, Budget, and Evaluation), and ad hoc representatives from the Office of the Health Education and Welfare Assistant Secretary for Planning and Evaluation.

The Office of Education identified three categories in which research might be directed (Education Division, U.S. Department of Health, Education, and Welfare, Proposed Research Plan for Bilingual Education, July, 1979):

A. Investigation of various national needs for bilingual education;
B. Research to improve the effectiveness of services for students; and
C. Research and evaluation to improve the management and operation of the Title VII programs.

Under the rubric of efforts to improve services (B), the following research studies were specified:

- studies to determine and evaluate effective models of bilingual-bicultural programs;
- studies to determine language acquisition characteristics and the most effective method of teaching English (in a bilingual-bicultural program);
- a 5-year longitudinal study [on the effectiveness of this title];
- studies [on] . . . methods of [identifying children needing services];
- studies [on] . . . teaching reading to Limited English Proficient (LEP) children and adults;
- studies of . . . teaching about culture.

As the research agenda was being formulated by the Part C Committee, the proposed federal regulations regarding remedies to *Lau* violations were finally published in the *Federal Register* on August 5, 1980, during the final months of the Carter administration. The proposed *Lau* regulations went even further than the earlier remedies, mandating bilingual education in schools with more than 25 LEP students from the same language group. However, the change in administration brought an immediate change in the government's approach. The new Secretary of Education in the Reagan administration, Terrel Bell, withdrew the proposed regulations on February 2, 1981, calling them "harsh, inflexible, burdensome, unworkable, and incredibly costly" and criticizing federal mandates for native language instruction as "an intrusion on state and local responsibility" (quoted in Crawford, 1989, page 42).

The Reagan administration was hostile to bilingual education. President Reagan, for example, early in his first term, declared: "It is absolutely wrong and against American concept to have a bilingual education program that is now openly, admittedly, dedicated to preserving their native language and never getting them adequate in English so they can go out into the job market" (New York Times, March 3, 1981). This statement by President Reagan suggests that the preservation and use of native language and the neglect of teaching English occur together in bilingual education programs. This is by no means the case.

An influential document in the early years of the administration was an internal staff study written at OPBE and later published (Baker and de Kanter, 1983). The study had been undertaken at the request of the Carter administration's White House Regulatory Analysis and Review Group in relation to its proposed regulations. The study, completed in September 1981, reviewed evaluation reports from 39 transitional bilingual education programs. The authors believed these programs offered valid comparisons with alternative programs (ESL and structured immersion), and concluded that there was insufficient evidence to warrant the prescription of bilingual education. The authors called for flexibility and better designed studies (Baker and de Kanter, 1983, page 52):

> The low quality of the methodology found throughout the literature is a serious problem. Studies have evidenced a lack of random assignment between treatment and control groups, the use of study designs that cannot show a treatment effect in the absence of random assignment, and a failure to apply appropriate statistical tests to demonstrate program effects.

Neither the Baker and de Kanter study nor the earlier AIR study were subjected to independent review prior to dissemination, and many serious questions have been raised about them (see, e.g., Willig, 1987).

By the time the Bilingual Education Act was up for reauthorization in 1984, the questions raised by the AIR study and the Baker and de Kanter document, in conjunction with a decidedly different political climate in Washington, paved the way toward allowing flexibility in how funds were awarded. Specifically, a compromise was struck in which 4 to 10 percent of the total bilingual education funding could be used towards Special Alternative Instructional Programs (SAIP)—programs that do not use the native language.

William Bennett, the new Secretary of Education, focused national attention on bilingual education on September 26, 1985, in a well-publicized address, at which he said (cited in Crawford, 1989, page 71): "After $1.7 billion of Federal funding, we have no evidence that the children whom we sought to help—that the children who deserve our help—have benefited." He called for an initiative to remove the cap on SAIP and advocated greater flexibility and local control. The proposed changes were published in the November 22, 1985, issue of the Federal Register.

The political battle over program flexibility in funding continued into the 1988 reauthorization, in which up to 25 percent of funds for programs were made available for SAIP. Intervening in this conflict was a controversial General Accounting Office report (U.S. General Accounting Office, 1987) requesting expert evaluation of the validity of claims made by the Department of Education regarding the lack of evidence on the effectiveness of bilingual education. The report concluded that there was research evidence to support bilingual education and questioned the basis of claims made by Secretary Bennett and other department officials. The report served as a counterweight against the strong claims made by the critics of bilingual education. Also relevant in the funding formula debate was the leak of an interim report on the first-year scores from the Immersion Study in June, 1986, in which unadjusted scores showed the English immersion group scoring lower than the other two groups in most of the measures. It was evident that there were high stakes involved in the results from this study.

It is critically important for the design and implementation of any intervention study (more generally, any intervention) that the objectives (goals) of the treatments be clearly delineated. At least two possibly conflicting objectives of bilingual education are to (1) minimize the time required to learn English and to (2) maximally facilitate the learning of basic skills, of which English proficiency is only one component.

Neither these, nor any other clearly stated objectives, are listed in the legislation for bilingual education, the legal cases associated with it, or in the studies under review. *The lack of clearly stated objectives* makes any claims of effectiveness, or lack thereof, particularly of teaching approaches, exceedingly difficult to interpret, regardless of the specific data being discussed or the variables used in the claimed assessment of effectiveness.

In Appendix A we provide a brief history of bilingual education in the United States. That material is excerpted from the report *The Condition of Bilingual Education in the Nation: A Report to Congress and the President* (U.S. Department of Education, 1991). We also present a chronology of important events in bilingual education policy.

THE PRESENT STUDIES

The two studies under review in this report were both initiated within the Department of Education through requests for proposals (RFPs) issued by the Part C Coordinating Committee in 1982. It is notable that this occurred shortly after the collapse of the *Lau* regulations as proposed by the Carter administration, as well as the circulation of the Baker and de Kanter report, and there was increasing uneasiness about the prescription of the use of the native language.

Because it was an interagency policy body, the actions of the Part C Committee might be seen partly as the result of compromises between competing interests. For example, the National Institute of Education (NIE) valued basic research on learning and bilingualism, as well as classroom-based research. Most of the field-initiated research on bilingual education during this period was monitored by this agency: during the 1979–1981 fiscal years, NIE project officers monitored a set of seven studies under the title of "Significant Bilingual Instructional Features" that were funded for a total of over $4 million (National Clearinghouse for Bilingual Education Forum, 1982). The purpose of these studies was to identify instructional

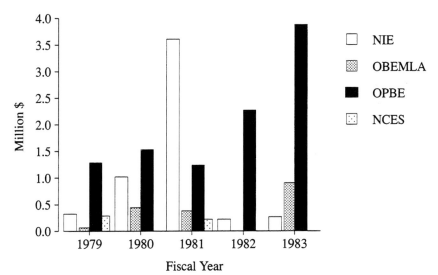

FIGURE 1-1 Part C Funds, 1979-1983

features in classrooms with minority-language students and to understand the linguistic, cognitive, and social processes involved.

An analysis of the shift of Part C funds over time is seen in Figure 1-1. Between 1981 and 1982, research priorities shifted from NIE-funded basic research studies to evaluation studies funded OPBE. The two studies under review in this report were funded principally by OPBE, and accounted for a substantial portion of the funds available in 1982 and 1983.

The Longitudinal Study

It is noteworthy that the RFP for the National Longitudinal Study begins with apparent reference to the AIR and Baker and de Kanter documents:

> Previous evaluations of the effectiveness of services provided to language minority limited English proficient students have focused narrowly and by design on selected subpopulations of students and selected services provided. One example of such an evaluation was the 2-year longitudinal study of ESEA Title VII-funded Spanish/English bilingual education projects, completed in 1978 and funded by the U.S. Department of Education. More recently, an attempt to synthesize results from diverse research studies demonstrated again the importance of complete documentation of service, school, child, and home characteristics for drawing conclusions about service effectiveness. Although in the past such evaluations may have been appropriate for the Department, this is not the case now. For the Department to formulate federal education policy regarding services provided to language minority limited English proficient students in a time of decreasing federal monies and regulation, a comprehensive information base is required—a base containing information about the broad range of services being provided to such students.

The RFP also makes note of the basic research studies, including the studies funded by NIE on significant instructional features:

> Collectively, these studies are considered by the Department to constitute part of a comprehensive approach to better understanding problems and potential solutions to providing appropriate educational services to language minority limited English proficient students in the United States. Additionally and importantly, the results of these studies provide a significant part of the foundation which the Department has considered essential before a major evaluation of the effectiveness of a broad range of services provided such students could be successfully undertaken. The Department now believes that the prerequisite foundation is in place and is therefore initiating a national longitudinal evaluation of the effectiveness of services provided language minority limited English proficient students in the United States.

In fact the study did not result in an evaluation of a set of distinct program alternatives, about which much was known as a result of basic research. As noted later in this report, the study suffered from a key failing: *the programs that it was intended to evaluate did not generally exist in well-defined form, making their evaluation very problematic.* The analyses that were eventually conducted were not a definitive evaluation, but, rather, an attempt to find characteristics of programs that showed evidence of being effective.

The Immersion Study

The RFP for the Immersion Study draws text, at times verbatim, from the Baker and de Kanter report. Notably absent are any references to other research funded by the Part C Committee.

The tensions between the different agencies participating in the Part C Committee were known to many researchers in the field who received their funds from it. Because of difficulties encountered by NIE during this period, the competition over priorities for projects increasingly focused on OBEMLA rather than OPBE. As witnessed by the distribution of funds in 1983, OPBE had clearly become dominant in the process.

Administrative Arrangements for the Studies

Administratively, OPBE started and maintained control of the Immersion Study. For the Longitudinal Study, however, control shifted between OPBE and OBEMLA. The panel reviewed a number of documents and memoranda written by the contractors for the Longitudinal Study that referred to organizational disputes regarding which agency was actually in charge and how this affected the work of the study.

OVERVIEW OF THE PANEL'S REPORT

The Panel to Review Evaluation Studies of Bilingual Education was convened to report on the two particular studies: *The National Longitudinal Study of the Evaluation of the Effectiveness of Services for Language-Minority Limited-English-Proficient Students* (Burkheimer et al., 1989) and *The Longitudinal Study of Immersion Strategy, Early-exit and Late-exit Transitional Bilingual Education Programs for Language-Minority Children* (Ramirez et al., 1991a, 1991b). A major charge to the panel was to suggest alternative ways of conducting evaluation studies.

The issues of appraising the studies at hand and providing advice for future studies are inexorably intertwined. Throughout this report the panel mixes advice and questions about future studies with a critical evaluation of the Longitudinal and Immersion Studies. When there was a choice between specific comments on one of the studies or general comments about evaluation studies, the panel has chosen the latter path, using specific comments as examples.

Chapter 2 sets the theoretical stage for a careful statistical discussion of the two studies and introduces definitions and examples of statistical and experimental terminology.

The heart of this report consists of Chapters 3 and 4, which present the panel's appraisals of the Longitudinal Study and Immersion Study, respectively. Both of the chapters also present quotations that show the Department of Education's official view of these studies. Much of the substance in these chapters speaks directly to the two studies, but each chapter also offers general comments on conducting evaluation studies. Both chapters offer specific suggestions for future analyses of the reported data. Although the panel has attempted to make these chapters self-contained, there are inevitable references to the final reports of the two studies. Readers who have no knowledge of the appraised reports should still be able to understand the discussion in these chapters. As the two studies were very different in intent and execution, so the two chapters reflect very different statistical and substantive concerns, but the general methodology and statistical concerns in the two chapters are complementary.

Chapter 5 continues the discussion of the design of bilingual education studies that begins in Chapter 2 but focuses on the need for underlying theories. The panel believes that explicit theories of education, including explicit objectives, are required to both motivate and structure the sensible statistical design of studies to evaluate alternative forms of education. For example, the primary objectives of bilingual education in the United States remain controversial. It is imperative that there be clear and agreed upon statements of the goals of bilingual (or other) education programs before one attempts to assess the impact of different programs.

Once there is an explicit set of goals there also need to be theories that suggest how to achieve those goals. The theories may be based on exploratory studies, examination of existing studies, or other methods. Only after a theory is articulated can one begin to define interventions, measurement tools, and design strategies. Just as important is the concern about how to measure the postulated effects, who the subjects will be, and how the interventions might differentially effect different subject populations.

There is a tension between the need for broad studies that are applicable to a general population and narrowly focused studies that are likely to find specific effects. The panel strongly believes that it is much better to find out what works somewhere than to fail to find what works anywhere. Without proper statistical designs, most intervention studies are likely to fail. A reasonable strategy is to attempt to sequentially accumulate knowledge about programs through focused, designed, and controlled experiments; when possible, it is better to perform contolled experiments than observational studies.

The panel's conclusions and recommendations are presented in Chapter 6. This chapter is partitioned into a section of conclusions about each study and a general set of conclusions and recommendations. The panel highlights the major weaknesses in the studies and provide specific recommendations on how to avoid similar weaknesses in future studies.

The appendices provide some background material on bilingual education in the United States, a technical summary of a statistical methodology used in the Immersion Study, a list of acronyms used in the report, and biographical sketches of the panel and staff.

REFERENCES

Atkinson, R., and Jackson, G., eds. (1992) *Research and Education Reform: Roles for the Office of Educational Research and Improvement.* Committee on the Federal Role in Education Research, Commission on Behavioral and Social Sciences and Education, National Research Council. Washington, D.C.: National Academy Press.

Baker, K. A., and de Kanter, A. A., eds. (1983) *Bilingual Education: A Reappraisal of Federal Policy.* Lexington, Mass.: Lexington Books.

Burkheimer, Jr., G. J., Conger, A. J., Dunteman, G. H., Elliott, B. G., and Mowbray, K. A. (1989) Effectiveness of services for language-minority limited-english-proficient students (2 vols). Technical report, Research Triangle Institute, Research Triangle Park, N.C.

Crawford, J. (1989) *Bilingual Education: History, Politics, Theory, and Practice.* Trenton, N.J.: Crane Publishing Co.

Dannoff, M. N. (1978) Evaluation of the impact of ESEA Title VII Spanish/English bilingual education programs. Technical report, American Institutes for Research, Washington, D.C.

Fishman, J. A. (1977) The social science perspective. In *Bilingual Education: Current Perspectives. Vol. 1: Social Science*, pp. 1–49. Rosslyn, Va.: Center for Applied Linguistics.

Hakuta, K. (1986) *Mirror of Language: The Debate on Bilingualism.* New York: Basic Books.

Lambert, W. E. (1980) Two faces of bilingualism. In *Focus, No. 3*. Rosslyn, Va.: National Clearinghouse for Bilingual Education.

Lambert, W. E. (1992) Pros, cons, and limits to quantitative approaches in foreign language research. In B. F. Freed, ed., *Foreign Language Acquisition Research and the Classroom*, chapter 19, pp. 321–337. Lexington, Mass.: D. C. Heath and Co.

National Clearinghouse for Bilingual Education Forum (1982) Update: Part C bilingual education research. National Clearinghouse for Bilingual Education, Rosslyn, Va.

Ramirez, D. J., Yuen, S. D., Ramey, D. R., and Pasta, D. J. (1991a) Final report: Longitudinal study of structured-english immersion strategy, early-exit and late-exit transitional bilingual education programs for language-minority children, Volume I. Technical report, Aquirre International, San Mateo, Calif.

Ramirez, D. J., Pasta, D. J., Yuen, S. D., Billings, D. K., and Ramey, D. R. (1991b) Final report: Longitudinal study of structured-english immersion strategy, early-exit and late-exit transitional bilingual education programs for language-minority children, Volume II. Technical report, Aquirre International, San Mateo, Calif.

Swain, M. (1992) French immersion and its offshoots: Getting two for one. In B. F. Freed, ed., *Foreign Language Acquisition Research and the Classroom*, chapter 19, pp. 321–337. Lexington, Mass.: D. C. Heath and Co.

U.S. Department of Education (1991) *The Condition of Bilingual Education in the Nation: A Report to the Congress and the President*. Office of the Secretary. Washington, D.C.: U.S. Department of Education.

U.S. General Accounting Office (1987) Bilingual education: A new look at the research evidence. Briefing Report to the Chairman, Committee on Education, Labor, House of Representatives, GAO/PEMD-87-12BR.

Willig, A. (1987) Meta-analysis of selected studies in the effectiveness of bilingual education. *Review of Educational Research*, 57(3), 351–362.

2

Research Methodology and Bilingual Education

DETERMINING CAUSES

Statistics is often thought of as a body of methods for learning from experience. The standard repertoire of statistical methods includes techniques for data collection, data analysis and inference, and the reporting of statistical results. Just as some experiences are more informative than others, some statistical techniques for data collection are more valuable than others in assisting researchers and policy makers in drawing inferences from data. The two studies reviewed by the panel used quite different statistical methodologies, although the methodologies fit within a common framework. An appreciation of this framework is essential to an understanding of the panel's evaluation of the two studies.

This chapter reviews some of the basic techniques for the collection of statistical data, the definition of outcomes and treatments, the units of analysis, and the kinds of inferences that are appropriate. In essence, there is a hierarchy of approaches to data collection: the more rigorous the design for data collection and the control of the setting under study, the stronger the inferences that can be made from the data that result about the universe of interest. Users of statistical methods often wish to draw causal conclusions, for example, from programs to achievement outcomes. This is especially true in a policy setting. If one concludes that when a school follows approach X to bilingual education, the performance and achievement of the students will be Y, one is claiming, at least in a loose sense, that X "causes" Y. The notion of which designs allow conclusions about the causal effects of treatments is critical to an appreciation of the evaluation of alternative bilingual education programs. Chapter 4 on the Immersion Study provides a focused discussion of a design-based approach to causal inference; here we present a general introduction to the topic.

There are no *general* sufficient conditions that can be used to declare and defend a claim that X "causes" Y. The evidence used to support such claims varies substantially with the subject matter under investigation and the technology available for measurement. Statistical methodology *alone* is of limited value in the process of inferring causation. Furthermore, consensus on causality criteria evolves over time among practitioners in different scientific lines of inquiry. A clear statement of the evidential base that should support claims that a particular treatment will be "effective" for English-language training in a bilingual education setting has not been put forth. For a historical discussion of the evolution of causality criteria in the setting of infectious diseases, see Evans (1976). For a discussion along similar lines in the social sciences, see Marini and Singer (1988). Nonetheless, throughout this chapter and the rest of this report the panel uses the word "causal" in its more narrow statistical or technical sense, fully realizing that in some cases such usage may violate the broader scientific meaning.

As part of the development of the evidential base leading to a claim that X causes Y, it is useful to distinguish between confirmation studies, whose purpose is to confirm a prior hypothesis, and discovery studies, whose purpose is to discover candidate mechanisms. For confirmation studies one introduces candidate causes in an intervention study (possibly randomized) whose objective is to evaluate the effects. For discovery studies, one starts from effects and carries out investigations whose objective is the determination of candidate causes. *Both forms of studies are necessary in the context of bilingual education.*

In a typical discovery study one analyzes what are regarded as successful intervention studies and asks what the underlying mechanism(s) was (were) that led to success. This is usually an analysis of multiple case studies in which one is looking for common features that led to success (effectiveness). In the process of discovering candidate causes that could be responsible for observed effects, one frequently infers that a complex cause—consisting of multiple interventions acting together—is really driving the system. It may be exceedingly difficult to determine the relative contribution of each intervention acting alone; however, in many instances whether one can isolate components may not even be a useful question to address. The key to devising a real-world intervention is simply the identification of the cluster of interventions that need to be simultaneously applied to produce the desired effects. A confirmatory intervention study should then use the full cluster of interventions as a treatment. This important scientific strategy must confront a political environment in which different parties have vested interests in demonstrating the effectiveness of their intervention acting by itself. There are a variety of methods for gathering information about bilingual education, including case studies and anecdotes, sample surveys, observational studies, and experiments or field trials. Another source of information is expert opinion, but we exclude that from our definition of data.

SOURCES OF DATA

Case Studies and Anecdotes

The careful study of a single case often allows for a rich contextual picture of circumstances surrounding some activity or event of interest. The event may be the legislative history of a bilingual education act in California or it may be the immersion experiences of students in a particular sixth grade classroom in Taos, New Mexico, in 1985–1986. The technical term for such a study or observation is a *case study.* Anecdotal evidence is usually less comprehensive than a formal case study: it may consist of informal comments by observers or through a "Suggestion Box"—soliciting comments at the end of an opinion survey. In medical research, carefully documented case studies of small groups of patients provide preliminary evidence that may contribute to understanding how successful a treatment is. Experts often use the case-study method to consider the special features of events and subsequently build a body of knowledge by the accumulation of cases.

Every field has its own pattern for case studies, based on experience and theory, and the field of bilingual education is no exception For example, Samaniego and Eubank (1991) carried out several case studies examining how an ambitious California experiment in bilingual education affected English proficiency. They used linear and logistic regression analyses to develop school specific profiles of students who successfully transferred skills developed in their first language into skills in the second language. Two profiles illustrate the diversity. One school consisted entirely of Spanish-speaking students who had never attended school in the United States. These students studied at this school (in Spanish) for just 1 year before transferring to other elementary schools in the district. A second site was a rural school whose student body was mostly children of agricultural workers. This school had early "mainstreaming" in subjects such as art, music, and physical education and more gradual mainstreaming in other subjects. These case studies suggested the presence of strong contextual effects: that is, outcomes were strongly affected by factors other than when and how mainstreaming occurred, such as the quality of an individual teacher.

Case studies often provide the starting point for research investigations by helping to define treatments and outcomes, as well as assisting in determining how to measure them in the discovery mode described above. This information, however, usually comes from a variety of sources of unknown reliability and with unknown biases. Consequently, it is difficult to generalize from a case study, since the data are collected in a manner not necessarily grounded in any *formal* rules of inference.

Sample Surveys

When the purpose of a study is to provide a systematic description of a large number of programs, institutions, or individuals, a case-study approach will simply not do. Although the collection of many cases provide more reliable information than a single case, a major issue is often how to generalize to other circumstances. Individual cases require some form of systematic selection in order to allow for the possibility of generalization. One way to gather information systematically in a manner that allows for generalization is through *sample surveys*.

Through surveys, investigators are able to ask questions about facts and quantities as they currently exist, recollections and records about past circumstances, and relationships among them. Thus, one might do a survey of schools and ask the principals questions about the bilingual and other language education programs in place and about the students enrolled in those programs. One might even record information about individual students. By reinterviewing the principals or the students several months or years later, one might add a *longitudinal* dimension to the survey, thus allowing for the study of how quantities and relationships have changed over time. In such longitudinal surveys the investigator does not seek to change the values of variables (for example, to influence the kinds of language programs at the school or the teacher training and support for those programs, in order to see what effects such changes might make). Rather, the investigator seeks to record information on a sample of schools or a sample of students in order to learn how things are changing.

The sampling aspect of a survey provides the mechanism for generalizing from the units at hand: for example, from the students in six school districts in Cook County, Illinois, to some larger population of interest, such as all elementary students in the state of Illinois. The latter is usually referred to as a *target* population. In a well-designed probability sample, the investigators can make inferences about occurrences in the population from the sample information. The term *representative* sample is often used in reports and accounts of sample surveys in the public press. As Kruskal and Mosteller (1988) note, however, the term has no precise meaning and thus the panel avoids the use of that term in this report.

Many large-scale surveys, such as the one described in Chapter 3 on the Longitudinal Study, use a complex form of random selection that involves the *stratification* and *clustering* of the units under investigation. Each unit in the population typically has a nonzero probability of being included in the sample. This probability can be determined in advance. In this sense, sample surveys allow for *external validity*, that is, for the generalization from sample to population. Several issues affect the ability to make inferences from a sample to a population of interest:

- the nonresponse rate in the sample (that is, what proportion of the originally designated sample units actually participated in the survey);
- the extent of missing data;
- in a longitudinal survey, the attrition rate of sample respondents over time; and
- the factual accuracy of responses.

External validity in data collection and analysis is often not sufficient for policy purposes. When an investigator wants to compare the effects of different treatments or programs, a sample survey has major weaknesses, even if the treatments or programs are in use in the population under study. *The major difficulty has to do with how the individuals were assigned to the treatments or programs in the first place.* If assignment is perfectly related to (or totally confounded with) the outcome of interest, then even the very best sampling scheme will not allow the investigator to sort out what treatment causes what outcome. For example, if students with greater academic or language-learning ability are placed in certain bilingual immersion programs, then the outcome that these students perform better in both languages may be attributable to the assignment mechanism and not the program itself. As a specific example, the Late-exit Program of the Immersion Study (see Chapter 4) used teachers with better training and more enthusiasm for the program. As those teachers differed systematically from teachers in other programs, the effects of the program itself cannot be disentagled from the effects of the teachers. To understand the effect of treatments on outcomes, one needs a stronger design, one that allows for the control of the assignment mechanism. (Sometimes statisticians speak of assigning treatments to subjects and other times of assigning subjects to treatments. The two are essentially equivalent concepts, and we use them interchangeably, depending on the context.)

Observational Studies

Sample surveys are a form of *observational study* involving a collection of cases. As noted above, in observational studies the investigator does not change the values of variables such as the treatments applied to individuals, but rather compares groups of individuals for which the values already differ.

The information from the case studies in the Samaniego and Eubank (1991) bilingual study, referred to above, could be regarded as an observational study with a small sample size (four or five schools, depending on definitions). The investigators fit separate regression models at each of the schools to adjust for differences across students. Their principal finding from the regressions was that there were quite different learning dynamics in different settings.

Observational studies are most naturally suited to drawing descriptive conclusions or statements about how groups differ. However, investigators and policy makers are often interested in why the differences occur. That is, they wish to draw inferences about the causal mechanisms responsible for observed differences and make policy recommendations based on the causal conclusions. Borrowing terminology from the literature on experiments, one often refers to treatment groups (groups that have received an intervention of policy interest) and control groups (groups that have received no treatment or the standard treatment). Descriptive inference draws conclusions about how the treatment and control groups differ. Causal inference attempts to attribute these differences to the treatment itself.

In an observational study the investigator does not control how the treatments are applied, but must simply observe units that have received the treatments as they occur naturally. This lack of control over assignment to treatments makes it difficult to draw unambiguous causal inferences from observational studies. The problem is that there is no way to ensure that the difference in treatments is the only relevant difference between treatment and control groups. *Selection bias* is the term used to describe the situation in which the variables that affect the response also affect whether or not the intervention is received. Selection bias must be a major concern of any investigation that seeks to draw causal conclusions from observational data. For example, suppose that a study seeks to discern differences between public and private school students. One question of interest is how much better or worse public school students would do if they were assigned to a private school. An outcome (measured response) is a test score, and the conceptual intervention is assignment to a private school rather than a public school. The study, however, is observational because the students are not assigned to private or public schools, but choose one or the other, presumably on the basis of individual characteristics that may or may not be known to, and observed by, the investigator. A simple statistical model to describe the response variables in this study is as the sum of three parts: (1) the effect of assignment to a private school (intervention effect); (2) an innate ability; and (3) a randomly distributed statistical error. The average response for private school students is the intervention effect plus average innate ability. The average response for public school students is simply average innate ability. Thus, at first blush, it seems that the difference between average responses for private and public school students is the effect of being assigned to a private school.

The problem is that the average innate ability of private school students may not be the same as that of public school students. Innate ability may affect whether a student goes to a private school. If it were possible to predict innate ability through some surrogate, such as family income, *without error*, then one could discern the intervention effect. Clearly, this is not possible. Alternatively, one could determine the intervention effect through random assignment to the intervention: see the role of random assignment in experiments below.

Analyses that takes explicit account of the process of self-selection into public versus private schools, or more general selection processes, are an essential ingredient of assessments (in observational studies) of alternative treatments. For a discussion of the basic ideas in modeling processes of selection, see Cochran (1965).

Experiments and Quasi-Experiments

In a study of the effect of an intervention, the intervention may or may not be controlled by the investigator. In a study with a controlled intervention, there are usually secondary, intervening, or confounding variables that may affect the results but are not themselves of primary interest. These confounding effects must be allowed for, either in the design or in the analysis of the study. Inference is necessarily based on a model, whether implicit or explicit, that describes how the secondary variables affect the results. Either the model is known or is not known but is assumed. This is a fuzzy distinction. A better distinction would be whether or not the model is widely accepted in scientific communities. When a model is established by the design of the study, the distinction is clear, and there is common acceptance that the model is known. Two common ways in which a model is established by design are when levels of secondary variables are predetermined and controlled for the desired inference and when the intervention is randomly assigned, thereby forming a group of those selected to receive the intervention to be compared with those who have not been selected. In both of these situations, the secondary variables do not have to be measured or adjusted for. Moreover, with randomization, the secondary variables do not even need to be identified.

If the intervention in a study is controlled by the investigator and the model that describes the effects of secondary variables is known, as is the case with randomization, the study is an *experiment.* The term *quasi-experiment* pertains to studies in which the model to describe effects of secondary variables is not known but is assumed. It applies to either observational studies or studies with controlled interventions but without randomization.

One widely used example of a quasi-experiment involves an interrupted time series, with observations before and after the "interruption." In that context, "before" serves as a control for "after," and the difference is used to measure the effect of the treatment that is applied during the interruption. When change is at issue, one needs multiple time series, with an interruption in one or more of the series, but not in the others. Quasi-experiments allow for stronger causal inferences than do uncontrolled observational studies. They fall short of randomized controlled experiments as the study of choice for causal purposes. In the interrupted time-series example, if it is a change in the prior conditions that produces the interruption, it is a serious concern.

In *controlled field trials* or *experiments*, the investigator explores what happens when treatments or programs are deliberately implemented or changed. An experiment is a carefully controlled study designed to discover what happens when variables are changed. In experiments, the process of randomization—that is, the random assignment of treatments to units or of units to treatments—is used to remove doubts about the link of the assignment to the outcomes of interest. There is a tension between balancing the treatments and controls with respect to other variables that may be correlated with the outcome and randomization in treatment assignment. Randomization provides for internal validity of the results of the experiment: that is, if one applied the treatments with a different randomization one would still expect to be able to make similar inferences to the collection of units in the experiment. External validity then allows for generalizations to some larger population. The issues of internal and external validity are treated in more detail in Campbell (1978).

Control in an experiment may be exercised not only over the implementation of the treatments, but also over other variables that might otherwise impede the ability of linking differences in outcome to differences in treatment. Control in the sense of coordination of a multisite experiment is of special relevance to experimental studies for educational policy.

As valuable as controlled experiments are, it is sometimes impossible to implement them, for practical or ethical reasons, and they are sometimes undesirable. For example, the treatments may simply not be assignable to all subjects. Offering an English/Spanish immersion program to all students may be of little value to those whose native tongue is Vietnamese. Yet having such students in a classroom may be unavoidable. Furthermore, many government funding bodies require that investigators gain the informed consent of participants in an experiment (or in the case of students, the informed consent of their parents). Understandable though this is, students' refusal to participate can undermine the integrity of the experiment. In the case of educational experiments, the cooperation of school boards, administrators, teachers, and parents is often required. Finally, resources may simply be inadequate to implement a carefully designed randomized experiment. Controlled experiments may, under certain circumstances, also be undesirable. A controlled experiment in a classroom may lead to significant and interesting results, but if the classroom intervention can not be generally applied, then the outcome may be useless.

One often settles for an observational study, without randomization, and typically without the various levels of control that are the hallmark of the well-designed randomized, controlled field trial. One must then attempt to identify confounding variables, measure them in the study, and then adjust for them to the extent possible in the analysis. This is a perilous enterprise, and it is often difficult to defend such a study against concerns about alternative causes or variables not measured or poorly measured. Confounding can also, but is less likely to, occur in randomized studies. For descriptions of some large-scale national social experiments in which these issues and concerns are discussed, see Fienberg, Singer, and Tanur (1985).

The Role of Randomization

Deliberate randomization provides an unambiguous probability model on which to base statistical inferences. Surveys typically use random selection of sample units from some defined population. Each population unit has a known, nonzero probability of being selected into the sample. These selection probabilities are used as the basis for generalizing the sample results to the population of interest. For example, a study might conclude that students in Program A scored on average 15 points higher than students in Program B. Often, this result is accompanied by a statement of confidence in the result; for example, that the difference in scores is accurate to within plus or minus 1 percentage point. The score difference in the sample is a matter of verifiable fact. Of more interest is the inference that scores in the population differ on average between 14 and 16 points. Randomization provides the theoretical basis for extending results from students whose scores have been measured to conclusions about students whose scores have not been measured. That is, in this context, randomization or random selection from a well-defined population provides external validity.

Experiments use random assignment to treatments in drawing inferences about the effect of treatments. Again, the observed difference between the treatment and control groups is a matter of verifiable fact, but one is really interested in what would have happened had the treatments been assigned differently (or, in what would happen if the treatments were assigned in similar circumstances at a future time). Randomization provides a theoretical basis for extending the sample results to conclusions about what would have happened to the units in the experiment if a different realization of the randomization had occurred. That is, randomization provides for internal validity.

Some statisticians are willing to generalize from samples in which selection was not random, as long as a plausible argument can be made that the results would be similar had selection been random. Thus, they would accept external validity in a population similar in important respects to the one studied, even if the sample units were not selected at random from that population. They might also accept internal validity for a study that could be argued to resemble a randomized experiment or for which they could build a defensible statistical model of the differences from a randomized experiment and use it to adjust for those differences.

Those involved with evaluation studies are legitimately concerned with both internal and external validity. Without external validity, one cannot tell whether a proposed policy would be effective beyond the specific units that have been studied. Without internal validity, one cannot even tell whether the proposed policy is effective in the group studied. Unfortunately, there is a tension between achieving internal and external validity. Generalizing to large populations (such as all school children in the United States) requires large studies, preferably with random selection of participating schools and districts. In such large studies, it is extremely difficult to exercise the controls required for internal validity. In smaller studies, it is much easier to achieve internal validity, but one generally cannot include all the subpopulations and sets of conditions of policy interest.

TREATMENTS AND OUTCOMES

Since the results of an evaluation study will depend critically on which outcomes are studied, it is important to define clearly the outcome of interest. In bilingual education there are a variety of possible outcomes, of which two are of particular interest: one is proficiency in English as soon as possible, and the other is proficiency in academic subjects—mathematics, English, reading, etc. The preferred bilingual education treatment may vary depending on the choice of outcome.

Treatment Definitions and Treatment Integrity

No matter how hard an investigator works to define the treatment to be applied in a given study, when the treatment is actually applied, changes tend to creep in. Over the course of a multiple-year immersion study, teachers may treat students differently than the program protocol requires. For example, if teachers expect a new program to be superior to the standard one, they may begin to change what they do in classrooms that are supposed to be implementing the standard program. This would change the treatment being applied to the control group and make it more difficult to find differences in outcomes among the groups under study. One of the lessons from medical experimentation is that a medicine prescribed is not necessarily a medicine actually used. Thus, for experiments in bilingual education, investigators must specify *a priori* exactly how the treatment or program is to be implemented and how they plan to monitor that implementation.

Distinguishing the Unit of Experimentation from the Unit of Analysis

There is an intimate link between the unit of randomization in an experiment and the unit of analysis. Suppose one assigns programs to schools but one measures outcomes on students. What does the randomization justify as the level of analysis for internal variability? The usual social science and educational research textbooks are often silent on this issue.

If one carries out the assignment of treatments at the level of schools, then that is the level that can be justified for causal analysis. To analyze the results at the student level is to introduce a new, nonrandomized level into the study, and it raises the same issues as does the nonrandomized observational study. This means that if one does an experiment with 10 schools organized into 2 districts of 5 each and if one randomly assigns Program X to District 1 and Program Y to District 2, then there are just 2 observations at the level of assignment even though there were thousands of students participating in the study.

The implications of these remarks are twofold. First, it is advisable to use randomization at the level at which units are most naturally manipulated. Second, when the unit of observation is "lower" than the unit of randomization or assignment of treatment, then for many purposes the data need to be aggregated in some appropriate fashion to provide a measure that can be analyzed at the level of assignment. Such aggregation may be as simple as a summary statistic or as complex as a context-specific model for association among lower-level observations. There are concerns, however, other than the validity of the randomization in designing and carrying out an analysis. Even when treatments have been randomized, it is sometimes desirable both for reasons of improved accuracy or because of the research questions being addressed in the study to statistically adjust for attributes of the units or to carry out the analysis at a lower level of aggregation than the units being randomized. An example of the former is in the RAND Health Insurance Experiment (Marquis et al., 1987) and of the latter in a randomized school-based drug prevention study (Ellickson and Bell, 1992). As this brief discussion suggests, there are tradeoffs in designing and carrying out valid evaluation studies.

DEVELOPING A RESEARCH AND EVALUATION PROGRAM

In undertaking a program of research and evaluation, it is important to distinguish three broad classes of objectives, labeled here as description, research, and evaluation. In general these classes of objectives require different types of study design, and there is an order among them: general descriptive and research studies must precede evaluation studies if there is to be a likelihood of success in conducting an evaluation.

A descriptive study is one for which the intention is to characterize the population and its subgroups. The descriptive component of the Longitudinal Study and, to a lesser extent, the descriptive phase of the longitudinal component of that study belong in this mode. They attempt to characterize the types of bilingual education programs available and the students and teachers who participate in them. One tries to design a descriptive study so that it is possible to generalize to the population of interest through the use of statistical methods. Before embarking on an evaluation study of a series of program types, it is essential to know about the programs actually in place and the extent of their implementation.

Research studies attempt to determine explicitly the relative effectiveness of specifically defined programs. Investigators often conduct studies in restricted populations and attempt to use experimental design features, such as randomization and matching. It is common practice to conduct research studies under relatively controlled conditions. These features enhance the ability of the studies to determine that the programs studied have had a real effect, and they can give an indication of the magnitude of such effects.

Evaluation studies attempt to ascertain the general effectiveness of broad classes of programs for the purposes of informing public policy. As with research studies, the use of controlled conditions and even randomization adds to their value. A given program or intervention is likely to vary from site to site with regard to the details of implementation, and an evaluation study often covers a variety of subpopulations. Thus, design of an evaluation study can be extremely difficult.

In an orderly world, one would expect a natural progression from description to research to evaluation. Yet in the real world, studies to evaluate the impact of policy decisions often proceed in the absence of careful research studies to inform policy.

REFERENCES

Hoaglin et al. (1982) and Mosteller, Fienberg, and Rourke (1983) provide elementary introductions to the types of statistical studies described in this chapter. Yin (1989) gives some formal ideas on the design and methodology of case-studies. Kish (1965) is a standard text for the design and analysis of complex sample sample surveys. Cochran (1965) and Rubin (1984) discuss the planning and analysis of observational studies and the devices that can be used to strengthen them for the purposes of causal inference. Cook and Campbell (1979) give a description of specific designs for quasi-experiments and Cox (1958b) provides a detailed introduction to randomized controlled experiments. For a detailed introduction to assorted topics in statistical studies and methods of analysis, see the encyclopedias edited by Kruskal and Tanur (1978) and Johnson and Kotz (1982–1989).

Campbell, D. T. (1978) Experiemental design: Quasi-experimental design. In W. H. Kruskal and J. M. Tanur, eds., *International Encyclopedia of Statistics*, pp. 299–304. New York: The Free Press.

Cochran, W. G. (1965) The planning of observational studies of human populations (with discussion). *Journal of the Royal Statistical Society, Series A*, 128, 124–135.

Cook, T. D., and Campbell, D. T. (1979) *Quasi-experimentation*. Chicago, Ill.: Rand McNally.

Cox, D. R. (1958b) *The Planning of Experiments*. New York: John Wiley.

Ellickson, P. L., and Bell, R. M. (1992) Challenges to social experiments: A drug prevention example. *Journal of Research in Crime and Delinquency*, 29, 79–101.

Evans, A. S. (1976) Causation and disease: The Henle-Kock postulates revisited. *Yale Journal of Biology and Medicine*, 49, 175–195.

Fienberg, S. E., Singer, B., and Tanur, J. (1985) Large-scale social experimentation in the united states. In A. C. Atkinson and S. E. Fienberg, eds., *A Celebration of Statistics: The ISI Centenary Volume*, pp. 287–326. New York: Springer Verlag.

Hoaglin, D. C., Light, R., McPeek, B., Mosteller, F., and Stoto, M. (1982) *Data for Decisions*. Cambridge, Mass.: Abt Associates.

Johnson, N. L., and Kotz, S., eds. (1982–1989) *The Encyclopedia of Statistical Sciences* (10 volumes). New York: John Wiley.

Kish, L. (1965) *Survey Sampling*. New York: John Wiley.

Kruskal, W. H., and Mosteller, F. (1988) Representative sampling. In S. Kotz and N. L. Johnson, eds., *Encyclopedia of Statistical Sciences*, volume 8, pp. 77–81. New York: John Wiley and Sons.

Kruskal, W. H., and Tanur, J. M., eds. (1978) *The International Encyclopedia of Statistics* (2 volumes). New York: Macmillan and the Free Press.

Marini, M. M., and Singer, B. (1988) Causality in the social sciences. In C. C. Clogg, ed., *Sociological Methodology 1988*, chapter 11, pp. 347–409. Washington, D.C.: American Sociological Association.

Marquis, W. G., Newhouse, J. P., Duan, N., Keeler, E. B., Leibowitz, A., and Marqui, M. S. (1987) Health insurance and the demand for medical care: Evidence from a randomized experiment. *American Economic Review*, 77, 252–277.

Mosteller, F., Fienberg, S. E., and Rourke, R. E. K. (1983) *Beginning Statistics with Data Analysis*. Reading, Mass.: Addison-Wesley.

Rubin, D. B. (1984) William G. Cochran's contributions to the design, analysis, and evaluation of observational studies. In P. S. R. S. Rao and J. Sedransk, eds., *W. G. Cochran's Impact on Statistics*, pp. 37–69. New York: Wiley.

Samaniego, F. J., and Eubank, L. A. (1991) A statistical analysis of California's case study project in bilingual education. Technical Report 208, Division of Statistics, University of California, Davis.

Yin, R. K. (1989) *Case-Study Research. Design and Methods* (revised ed.). Newbury Park, Calif.: Sage Publications.

3

The Longitudinal Study

OVERVIEW

In 1983 the Department of Education began a major multiyear study that came to be known as the "National Longitudinal Study of the Evaluation of the Effectiveness of Services for Language-Minority Limited-English-Proficient Students" (hereafter referred to as the Longitudinal Study). The study was commissioned in response to concerns about the lack of a solid research base on the effectiveness of different approaches to the education of language-minority (LM) students. The study was a direct response to a call from Congress, in the 1978 Amendments to the Elementary and Secondary Education Act, for a longitudinal study to measure the effectiveness of different approaches to educating students from minority language backgrounds.

Although the ultimate goal of the Longitudinal Study was to provide evaluations to inform policy choices, the Department of Education determined that an evaluation study required a firmer information base about the range of existing services. The study consisted of two phases. The first phase was descriptive of the range of services provided to language-minority limited-English-proficient (LM-LEP) students in the United States and was used to estimate the number of children in kindergarten through sixth grade (grades K–6) receiving special language-related services. The second phase was a 3–year longitudinal study to evaluate the effectiveness of different types of educational services provided to LM-LEP students. The Longitudinal Study itself consisted of two components, a baseline survey and a series of follow-up studies in the subsequent 2 years.

The study began late in 1982, and data collection for the descriptive phase occurred during the fall of 1983. The prime contractor was Development Associates, Inc. A subcontractor, Research Triangle Institute (RTI), assisted with survey design and sampling. The research design for the longitudinal phase was developed during the spring of 1983. Baseline data collection for the longitudinal phase occurred in the fall of 1984. Additional data were collected in the springs of 1985, 1986, and 1987. The original contract did not cover data analysis, and a separate contract for data analysis was issued in 1988 to RTI, the subcontractor on the original contract.

As a basis for comparing and contrasting the panel's analysis of the Longitudinal Study, we present first the summary prepared by the U.S. Department of Education (1991).

The National Longitudinal Evaluation of the Effectiveness of Services for Language Minority, Limited English-Proficient (LEP) Students
   A joint initiative by OBEMLA and the Office of Planning, Budget and Evaluation from 1982 to December 1989, this study examined the effectiveness of instructional services in relation to particular individual, home and school/district characteristics. The Department is planning to contract with the National Academy of Sciences to undertake a review of the quality and appropriateness of the methodologies employed both for data collection and analysis of the very rich database. Findings from the Descriptive Phase (1984–1987) include:

- The need for LEP services is not evenly distributed geographically across states and districts. Almost 70 percent of all LEP students resided in California, 20 percent in Texas, and 11 percent in New York.
- LEP students were found to be more disadvantaged economically than other students. Ninety-one percent of LEP students were eligible for free or reduced-price lunches compared to 47 percent of all students in the same schools.
- LEP students were found to be at-risk academically, performing below grade level in native-language skills as well as in English and other subjects, as early as first grade. However, mathematics skills are reported to be generally superior to language skills in either language.
- Most instruction of LEPs is provided in English, or a combination of English and the native language.
- There were significant problems with district and school procedures for entry and exit:
    - Almost half of the schools countered [*sic*] district policy and reported using one criterion for program entry.
    - The entry criteria that were used were of the less rigorous variety, such as staff judgment or oral language tests versus the required use of English reading/writing tests.
    - Schools with relatively small enrollments of LEP students (under 50) mainstreamed an average of 61 percent of LEP students, compared with 14 to 20 percent of LEP students mainstreamed in schools with relatively large LEP enrollments.
    - Eighty-two percent of districts placed no time limit on continued participation in the bilingual program.

- Instructional staff persons who speak and understand languages other than Spanish are rare. While 78 percent of LEP students were Spanish-speaking, 64 percent of schools with LEP students had more than one foreign language represented; the mean was 3.5 languages per school.

The results from the Longitudinal Study were disappointing to those interested in policy, and their interpretation remained controversial. First, the data did suggest *correlations* between policy-relevant variables and educational outcomes of policy interest; however, attribution of *causation* from the reported analyses is extremely problematic. Because the study was based on a sample survey, it does not provide the basis for inferring that differences in outcomes are due to differences in services provided, nor does it provide a warrant for inferences about the impact of proposed changes in policy. Second, despite the effort expended to develop a longitudinal database, only single-year analyses were performed.

The failure of a study of such magnitude to produce results even approximating those anticipated is understandably a cause for concern. The need remains for an information base to guide policy on bilingual education. This chapter addresses four issues that arise from the study and its disappointing outcomes:

1. What information was obtained as a result of the descriptive and longitudinal phases of the Longitudinal Study?
2. What were the reasons for the failure of the study to achieve its major objectives, and to what extent could the problems have been prevented?
3. Might useful information be obtained from further analyses of existing data?
4. How should the outcome of this study affect the design and implementation of future studies of this nature?

Following the timeline presented below the remainder of this chapter is divided into four sections. The first two cover the descriptive and longitudinal phases, respectively. An overview of the study design, analysis methods, and results is provided for each phase, followed by the panel's critique. The third discusses the prospects for further analyses of study data, while the fourth discusses the implications of the Longitudinal Study for the conduct of future observational studies by the Department of Education.

1968	Bilingual Education Act passed.
1974	ESEA Title VII expanded *Lau* v. *Nichols* decision. School districts must give special services to LM-LEP students.
September 1982	RFP for the Longitudinal Study.
Late 1982	Longitudinal Study begins.
Spring 1983	Pilot testing of forms for descriptive phase.
Fall 1983	Data collection for descriptive phase.
Spring 1984	*Longitudinal Study Phase of the National Evaluation of Services for Language-Minority Limited-English-Proficient Students: Overview of Research Design Plans for*, report by Development Associates, Inc. Describes

	plans for analyzing descriptive phase data.
Fall 1984	Initial data collection for longitudinal phase.
December 1984	*The Descriptive Phase Report of the National Longitudinal Evaluation of the Effectiveness of Services for Language-Minority Limited-English-Proficient Students*, report by Development Associates, Inc. and Research Triangle Institute. Reports final results of descriptive phase.
Spring 1985	Second data collection in year one.
Spring 1986	Year two data collection.
June 1986	Development Associates, Inc., *Year 1 Report of the Longitudinal Phase*.
Spring 1987	Year three data collection.
May 1988	Request for proposal issued for data analysis for the longitudinal phase
February 1989	*Descriptive Report: Analysis and Reporting of Data from the National Longitudinal Evaluation of the Effectiveness of Services for Language-Minority Limited-English-Proficient Students*, report by Research Triangle Institute. Considers which original study objectives could be addressed by study data.
April 1989	*Analysis Plan: Analysis and Reporting of Data from the National Longitudinal Evaluation of the Effectiveness of Services for Language-Minority Limited-English-Proficient Students*, report by Research Triangle Institute. Describes plans for analyzing longitudinal phase data.
1991	*Effectiveness of Services for Language-Minority Limited-English-Proficient Students*, report by Research Triangle Institute. Reports final results of longitudinal phase.

THE DESCRIPTIVE PHASE

Objectives

The descriptive phase of the Longitudinal Study had nine objectives:

1. To identify and describe services provided to LM-LEP students in Grades K–6;
2. To determine the sources of funding for the services provided;
3. To estimate the number of LM-LEP students provided special language related services in Grades K–6;
4. To describe the characteristics of students provided instructional services for LM-LEPs;

5. To identify and describe home and community characteristics associated with each major language group;
6. To determine the entry/exit criteria used by schools and school districts serving LM-LEP students;
7. To determine the relationship between services offered for LM-LEP students and services offered to students in adjoining mainstream classrooms;
8. To identify clusters of instructional services provided to LM-LEP students in Grades K–6; and
9. To obtain information useful in designing a longitudinal evaluation of the differential effectiveness of the identified clusters of services provided to LM-LEP students.

The first eight objectives are concerned with characterizing the population of LM-LEP students in elementary grades in U.S. public schools and describing the range and nature of special services provided to them. The ninth objective was to provide information to inform the design of the subsequent longitudinal phase of the study.

Study Design and Data Collection

The descriptive study was designed as a four-stage stratified probability sample. First-stage units were states; second-stage units were school districts, counties, or clusters of neighboring districts or counties; third-stage units were schools; and fourth-stage units were teachers and students.

The target population of students consisted of elementary-age LM-LEP students receiving special language-related services from any source of funding. The study used local definitions of the term "language-minority limited-English-proficient" whenever available. Thus, the criteria for classifying students as LM-LEP varied from site to site, and the term "LM-LEP student" used in reporting study results refers to a student classified locally as LM-LEP, *not* to any defined level of English proficiency. This variation in classification criteria affects interpretation of results. Appendix A includes information on the identification of LEP students, by state.

Ten states (those with at least 2 percent of the national estimated LM-LEP population) were included in the sample with certainty, and an additional 10 states were selected as a stratified random sample of the remaining states, with selection probability proportional to estimated size of the elementary-grade LM-LEP population in the state. The state of Pennsylvania was subsequently dropped because of the refusal of the Philadelphia school district to participate. School districts were stratified according to the estimated LM-LEP enrollment in their respective states, then sampled within strata with probability proportional to the estimated LM-LEP enrollment. Schools were selected with a probability proportional to the estimated LM-LEP enrollment.

Teachers and students were sampled only from schools with at least 12 LM-LEP enrollments in grades 1 or 3. All academic content teachers who taught

LM-LEP students in selected schools in grades 1 through 5 were selected for inclusion in the sample. A stratified random subsample of schools was selected for the student sample. Up to five first graders and five third graders were randomly selected from each school. Of the five students in each grade, two were from the predominant language-minority group at the school and three were from other language-minority groups if such students existed; otherwise students from the predominant language-minority group were substituted.

Site visits were made to districts with large LM-LEP enrollments, and mail or telephone interviews were used in the remaining districts. In visited districts, site visits were made to schools with moderate to large LM-LEP enrollments, and mail or telephone interviews were administered in the remaining schools. Teachers completed a self-administered questionnaire. Student-level data consisted of a questionnaire completed by teachers who taught the student and a questionnaire filled out by field staff from student records. A planning questionnaire provided data from school personnel for planning the longitudinal phase.

Analysis Methods

The Descriptive Phase Report (Development Associates, 1984a) did not document the nature and full extent of missing data. The overall response rate on each of the major study instruments was at least 81 percent. For LM-LEP students, the combined school and student response rate within schools was 87.2 percent. The student sample was drawn from a sample of 187 of the 335 schools from which teacher-level data were obtained. (These teacher-level data were obtained from 98 percent of the schools selected.) Of the 187 schools, 176 permitted a sample of students to be drawn (94.1 percent). Within these 176 schools, a student background questionnaire was completed by 1,665 LM-LEP students of 1,779 students selected (92.6 percent). Teacher data were obtained for 95.8 percent of those 1,665 students. However, no information is given on the extent of item nonresponse, that is, missing information for individual questions. Missing data were handled by excluding cases of item nonresponse from tabulations of single items. The report notes that this approach assumes that respondents and nonrespondents do not differ in ways affecting the outcome of interest. This approach also reduces the amount of data available for analysis.

The results are presented primarily in the form of tabulations and descriptive statistics (means, percentages, and distributions). The analysis methods used were standard and appropriate. Most analyses used sampling weights. This means that, in computing average values, the observations were weighted by the inverse of their probability of selection into the sample. When observations are sampled at unequal rates from subpopulations with different characteristics, use of sampling weights allows the sample results to be generalized to the target population. For the Longitudinal Study, the target population for some analyses consists of all LM-LEP students in grades 1–5 in the United States, excluding Pennsylvania. Other analyses are restricted to grade 1 and grade 3 students attending schools with at least 12 LM-LEP students at either grade 1 or grade 3.

Chapter 9 of the Descriptive Phase Report (Development Associates, 1984a) categorizes service patterns into service clusters, or "sets of instructional services provided to one or more LM-LEP students at a particular school or schools, . . . based on their most salient features," thereby defining clusters of similar types of service. *There is no description of the methodology used for the categorization.* It appears that the researchers tried a number of different categorizations and finally settled on a typology that "provided the most workable array." The report does not explain why the typology used was more "workable" than others that were considered.

In general, the statistical methods used to analyze the survey results were straightforward. The results were presented in tabular form. Some form of graphical presentation of the results would have been quite helpful as an aid to understanding. Of particular statistical interest would have been graphical displays of the multidimensional space of observations on the variables used to define the service clusters—see Chambers, Cleveland, Kleiner, and Tukey (1983) for an introductory description of multidimensional graphical methods.

Summary of Results

The Descriptive Phase Report tabulates a great many results relevant to the objectives of the study goals listed above. This section provides a brief summary of them.

There is a great deal of variation in the operational definition of a LM-LEP student from district to district, and from school to school in some districts. Of the school districts, 61 percent had an official definition for a LM-LEP student, and 75 percent reported setting official entry criteria for eligibility for special LM-LEP services. Some districts defined subcategories of LM-LEP students. Three main criteria for entry into LM-LEP services were used: (1) tested oral English proficiency; (2) judgment of student need by school or district personnel; and (3) tested proficiency in English reading or writing. There was also variation in the instruments and procedures used to measure entry criteria within these broad categories.

Because of the variation in the definition of limited-English proficiency, estimates of the number of LM-LEP students based on the Longitudinal Study are not directly comparable with estimates based on any study that uses a standard definition. Moreover, the definition of a LM-LEP student can vary from year to year within a single district as a result of administrative policy, legal requirements, or economic pressures. It is possible that in some districts the requirement to serve all students in need of special services led to a *definition* of LM-LEP students as those students for whom services were provided. These factors argue for extreme caution in extrapolating estimates of the numbers of LM-LEP students to years much later than 1983 because changes in how LM-LEP students were defined would invalidate the results. Based on the data from this study, there were estimated to be 882,000 students locally defined as LM-LEP in grades K–6 of public schools in the United States in the 1983–1984 school year.

Spanish is by far the most prominent native language among LM-LEP students, accounting for an estimated 76 percent of LM-LEP students in all schools and 78 percent in schools with LM-LEP enrollments of more than 12 LM-LEP students. No other language accounted for more than 3 percent of the students in schools with enrollments of more than 12 LM-LEP students. Southeast Asian languages were predominant in 14 percent of schools; 36 percent of schools had students from only one language group other than English; 3 percent of schools had 12 or more language groups. The average across all schools was 3.5 languages.

Third-grade LM-LEP students were a few months older than the national norms for their grade level. First graders were near the national norms. Both first-grade and third-grade students were rated by teachers as being below grade-level proficiency in mathematics, English language arts, and native language arts, but third-grade students were rated as being closer to grade-level proficiency. More third graders than first graders were rated equal or higher on English-language skills than native-language skills. Of grade K–6 LM-LEP students, 91 percent received free or reduced-price lunches (a measure of socioeconomic status), in comparison with 47 percent of all students in the same schools.

Most student characteristics in the report appear as aggregates across all language groups. The Spanish-speaking group is a large subpopulation, and these students tended to receive different services. It would therefore be of interest to see tabulations of student characteristic variables classified by native language. One reported result is that 64 percent of Spanish-speaking students were born in the United States, in comparison with no more than 28 percent from any other language group. It would be interesting to determine whether observed differences exist in other measured variables, such as free-lunch participation and subject-area proficiency.

The district survey results indicated that an estimated 97 percent of districts with LM-LEP students in grades K–6 offered special services to these students, although 12 percent of teachers judged that students needing services were not receiving them. The nine states with the highest LM-LEP populations provided services to a higher percentage of their LM-LEP students than states with lower LM-LEP populations. In all districts a goal of services was to bring LM-LEP students to a level of English proficiency needed to function in an all-English classroom. Most districts also stated the goal of providing other skills necessary to function in a public school classroom. Very few districts (15 percent) stated the goal of maintaining or improving native language proficiency.

Services were generally provided in regular elementary schools, either in mainstream classrooms or in specially designated classrooms. Students were often in classrooms containing both LM-LEP and English-language-background students. Instruction for LM-LEP students was usually slightly below grade level. Most Spanish-speaking students received instruction in English delivered in the native language, native language as an academic subject, and ethnic heritage; most other LM-LEP students did not.

The contractors defined five types of service cluster in terms of the following variables:

1. use of native language
2. special instruction in English
3. rate of transition
4. native language arts instruction, based on a narrative program description by school personnel
5. narrative program description by school personnel

The five types of clusters were called:

(A) native language primacy
(B) continued instruction in native language and English
(C) change in language of instruction, subdivided into

   (C1) slow transition and
   (C2) fast transition

(D) all English *with* special instruction in English, subdivided into

   (D1) with native language-proficient personnel and
   (D2) without native language-proficient personnel

(E) all English *without* special instruction in English, subdivided into

   (E1) with native-language-proficient personnel and
   (E2) without native-language-proficient personnel

Table 3–1 shows the estimated percentages of schools offering, and first-grade LM-LEP students receiving, each type. Clusters emphasizing use of the native language appeared predominantly at schools with Spanish-speaking LM-LEP students; schools with no Spanish-speaking LM-LEP students were very likely to offer cluster D.

There was great variation in the characteristics of teachers providing services to LM-LEP students. Sixty-three percent of districts required special certification for teachers of LM-LEP students; fewer than 35 percent of teachers had such certification. In a number of districts requiring certification, teachers were teaching with provisional certification or waivers. Approximately 60 percent of teachers had received some special training in teaching limited-English-proficient students. About half of the teachers could speak a language other than English; this other language was overwhelmingly Spanish. Overall, field researchers found a positive attitude in most schools toward serving the needs of LM-LEP students.

Panel Critique of the Descriptive Phase Study

The descriptive phase study was based on a national probability sample of students and teachers. The sample was obtained through a four-stage sampling process of selecting states, school districts within states, schools, and their students (all eligible teachers from a selected school).

TABLE 3–1   Schools Offering and First-Grade LM-LEP Students Receiving, Each Type of Service Cluster

Type of Service Cluster	% Schools		% Students
A	3		7
B	11		26
C	26		40
C1		20	
C2		6	
D	51		25
D1		13	
D2		38	
E	6		1
E1		2	
E2		4	

The procedures used to draw the sample were generally standard and appropriate given the stated objectives. The sampling of states was a nonstandard feature of the design, with the 10 states with the largest proportion of the national total of elementary LM-LEP students included with certainty (these states contain 83.5 of the elementary-school LM-LEP population, 92 percent of the Spanish LM-LEP population, and 64 percent of the non-Spanish LM-LEP population). Of these 10 states, Pennsylvania, with 1.9 percent of the LM-LEP population, effectively did not participate. A stratified sample of 10 states was drawn from the remaining 41 states. In aggregate, the sample accounts for 91 percent of the LM-LEP target population.

This method of selecting a first-stage sample of 20 states is unusual. The objectives of the study might have been better served by one of two alternative strategies. If it was important to limit the number of states to 20, then restricting the study to the 20 states containing the largest proportion of LM-LEP students might well have been more desirable. Such a sample would have contained 92.7 percent of the LM-LEP population and would have constituted a worthwhile study population in its own right. Conversely, making statistical inferences from a sample of 10 states to a population of 41 is hazardous due to the widely differing characteristics of states and their school districts.

Another sampling design would have treated school districts as the first-stage sampling unit and would have used the nation as a target population. This design would have led to less extreme variation in sampling weights. Most of the prominent national surveys of schools and students use districts or schools as the first stage of selection (e.g., the discussion of the National Education Longitudinal Study in Spencer and Foran (1991)).

The selection of districts within the selected states gave a total of 222 districts. A number of districts refused to participate, including two large ones—Philadelphia, Pa., and Buffalo, N.Y. Since Philadelphia was one of only two selections from the state of Pennsylvania, the whole state (a state selected with certainty) was dropped from the sample. This decision is illustrative of one of the disadvantages of using states as the first stage of selection. In some other cases, districts that refused to participate were replaced in the sample by others. Of the 23 districts that refused, 19 were replaced in the sample, giving a final sample of 218 districts. The planned number of districts and the level of district participation appear quite adequate for a study of this nature.

Within districts, the school selection procedure gave an initial selection of 536 schools with LM-LEP students. Fourteen of these schools refused to participate, and two were replaced in the sample. This is a high level of participation at the school level. Given that the sampling to the school level was carried out by sampling professionals using a variety of standard and recommended sampling procedures, with relatively few district and school refusals, the study sample gave a sound basis for characterizing U.S. schools with respect to their LM-LEP population and services.

The school sample was reduced prior to the selection of teachers and students. Initially, 342 schools were identified as having sufficient LM-LEP students. All eligible teachers from these schools were selected—a total of 5,213, of whom 4,995 responded. A subsample of 202 of the 342 schools was used for selecting students. Of these, 187 schools actually provided student data, with five LM-LEP students selected for each of grades 1 and 3. Field data collectors were responsible for drawing these samples, but they were not uniform in the applications of sampling rules. As a result, the expected student sample yield of 1,980 was not achieved. A total of 1,909 students were actually sampled, but it is impossible to determine from the documentation provided which of these were original selections and which were replacements resulting from parental refusals to participate.

The sample sizes, sampling procedures, and response rates for teachers and schools were at least adequate to provide a sound basis for inference from the data collected, although it would have been desirable to have rates calculated with and without replacements for refusals. Two points are worthy of special note. First, estimates based on data from teachers and students do not relate to the whole LM-LEP population, but only to that part of the population from schools that would have been deemed "viable" for the conduct of the Longitudinal Study. Such schools had 12 or more LM-LEP students in grades 1 or 3 and contained 82 percent of LM-LEP population. Second, the procedure for sampling students in the field was not well controlled. The reported problems appear to have been minor; thus, it was still possible to weight the data appropriately. However, in the longitudinal phase, the problems were so severe that the data could not be weighted.

The procedures for weighting the data were appropriate and are well documented in Appendix E of Development Associates (1984a). With the caveat concerning the population restriction for student-level data, the study sample appears to be adequate for making inferences from the sample, assuming that there were no major problems with data quality. One exception is that school-level data for grade 6 cannot be reliably projected to national totals and proportions, because the sample only represents those sixth grades contained in sampled schools that have any of the grades 1 through 5. (That is, there are no assurances that the population of sixth graders in schools that have none of grades 1–5 is the same as the population of sixth graders in schools that include as least one of grades 1–5. This may seem a minor point, but it speaks directly to the issue of comparability of populations.) The report notes that there is a distinct underrepresentation at grade 6, observed by comparing school-level data to district-level data, which were not subject to such bias.

The Longitudinal Study Descriptive Phase Report is deficient in that there is no description of the method of calculating sampling errors. Given the nature of the sample design, this issue is far from being completely straighforward. Section 2.5 of Development Associates (1984a) is entitled "Weighting Factors and Standard Errors," but the text of this section (and Appendix E, to which it refers) does not discuss the topic of standard errors at all. The panel assumes that this was just an oversight in reporting and that appropriate sampling error estimation procedures were used.

Although standard error estimates are reported for a number of key tables, the reporting of them could usefully be far more extensive than it is. Most of the tables in the report would be enhanced by the inclusion of standard errors accompanying the estimates presented. The accompanying text would often be enhanced by a reference to the significance of, or a confidence interval for, reported differences.

In general, the report does a satisfactory job of describing the decisions that were made to transform the reported data into operational variables and of explaining why the decisions were made. These decisions appear to have been very logically based and well researched. The result is that useful interpretations can be made from the complex mass of data that were collected.

One concern is the apparent discrepancy between district-level and school-level data regarding the number of LM-LEP students enrolled. This is discussed in the report, but is perhaps dismissed too readily. As the report states, for grade 6 enrollment the discrepancy is explainable by, and consistent with, the sampling frame of schools, which was such that national estimates for grade 6 cannot be obtained from the school-level data. The discrepancy observed at other grades for Category B states (those in the second level of sampling) is not similarly explainable. The implied claim in the report is that the discrepancy is attributable to sampling error. The computation behind this claim is based on the assumption that the school and district samples were independent, but this is not correct. On the contrary, the sampled schools were drawn from within the sampled districts. The resulting sets of estimates are no doubt highly correlated, and it seems very unlikely that the observed discrepancy is attributable to sampling error alone. Further investigation of the relationship between the school- and district-level data appears warranted in an effort to better understand the discrepancy in these fundamental sets of estimates.

One type of estimate included in Chapter 3 of Development Associates (1984a) appears to be based exclusively on assumptions with little support evident from either the study or elsewhere. Projecting the number of LM-LEP students to include those in private schools, which were not included in the study, appears to be poorly founded. The proportion and characteristics of students who are LM-LEP in private schools could easily be considerably different from those in public schools for many reasons. The study itself does not appear to provide any basis for projecting the results to include private schools.

From the report itself it is difficult to evaluate the quality of the data collected, although the breadth of data collected is described in Appendix C of Development Associates (1984a). One aspect of data quality that is particularly noteworthy, and is pointed out in the report, is the definition of a LM-LEP student. This is a fundamental concept for the evaluation of bilingual education programs.

Throughout the Longitudinal Study the definition of a LM-LEP student was local, and the results of all aspects of the Longitudinal Study must be interpreted with this in mind. The problem may be more serious than one would at first suspect. The study obtained information at the school level about the size of the population of students who were considered non-English dominant, that is, the predominant language used by the child was not English. As the authors point out, one might reasonably expect that LM-LEP students would constitute a proper subset of non-English-dominant students, yet in 18 percent of schools there were more LM-LEP students than non-English-dominant students, while in 37 percent of schools the numbers in these two groups were identical. Thus, the reader must question what is encompassed in different schools by the term LM-LEP. This raises issues about the target population. The presence of LM-LEP students gave schools access to funds to which they might not otherwise have been entitled and may have led to overestimates of LM-LEP students.

Questionnaires were used to collect data on district services, school LM-LEP characteristics, school services, teacher characteristics and LM-LEP instructional practices, student proficiencies in language and mathematics, student perceptions of LM-LEP instruction, and student background data. Although missing data problems in the descriptive phase were encountered, they do not appear to have been severe, particularly in comparison with those experienced during the longitudinal phase of the survey. The report does not document in detail the sources and problems of missing data. Section 2.5 of Development Associates (1984a) discusses the issue briefly but gives no quantitative or qualitative summary of the quality of the data collected.

In summary, the descriptive phase of the study presents a large set of data that can be reliably projected to the national population of locally defined LM-LEP students, or a large majority of it, without substantial problems of bias or imprecision with regard to the representativeness of the sample. The quality of the data itself is less clear.

THE LONGITUDINAL PHASE

Objectives

As stated by Development Associates (1986) the longitudinal phase of the study had two broad objectives:

- to determine the degree to which services provided are effective collectively in enabling LM-LEP students in grade levels 1 through 5 to function successfully in all-English-medium classrooms; and
- to determine which clusters of services are most effective under specific conditions.

Although the study included services provided to LM-LEP students regardless of source of funding, a major purpose was to provide information to guide policy decisions regarding the allocation of funding under Title VII of the Elementary and Secondary Education Act (ESEA). More specifically, the study initially proposed to address the following five questions that were of interest to Congress, the Department of Education, and the educational establishment (Development Associates, 1986):

A. What are the effects of the special services provided for LM-LEP students in Grades 1–5 in terms of the LM-LEP student's ability to function effectively in an all-English-medium classroom?

B. How do the various combinations of special services ("service clusters") provided for LM-LEP students in Grades 1–5 compare in terms of the effectiveness with which LM-LEP students subsequently can function in an all-English-medium classroom?

C. What are the characteristics of English-proficient recipients of special services for LM-LEP students, and how does the receipt of these services affect the academic performance of these students, overall and when analyzed in terms of language background?

D. What are the characteristics of LM-LEP students whose parents refuse to permit them to participate in special LM-LEP services, and how does the non-receipt of these services affect their academic performance?

E. What have been the consequences of ESEA Title VII policy and funding on provision of effective services for LM-LEPs?

These major study questions were broken down into more than 60 specific research questions to be addressed by the study. These objectives were revised after data collection. The revised set of objectives is presented below, in the section entitled "Longitudinal Study Research Questions," together with the breakdown of specific research questions. Objectives D and E were dropped entirely. Objective C was changed to focus on the effects on LM-LEP students of having non-LM-LEP students in the classroom. Objectives A and B were modified to address effects on learning of English rather than effects on the ability to function in an all-English classroom. These modifications presumably reflect the realization that the data collected did not support the more ambitious initial objectives. Still, depending on how one counts overlapping questions, about 25 research questions remained to be addressed. At the data analysis phase, these objectives were further revised and restricted.

It is clear both from the planning documents and the original and revised study objectives that the Department of Education was concerned with drawing causal inferences from the study. That is, the longitudinal portion of the study was intended not only to document *correlations* between predictor and criterion variables, but to attribute causal explanations to those correlations, as required to predict the effects of proposed policy alternatives. Although the study did document correlations between outcomes of policy interest and policy relevant variables, causal attribution is extremely problematic. The study has documented the existence of certain relationships among the measured variables, but the data do not support inferences about how direct manipulation of the policy-relevant variables would affect any outcomes of concern.

Many of the effects of concern to the study developed over a long period of time. In particular, students in programs emphasizing a slow transition from native-language use to English-language use are expected to show lower English-language proficiency in earlier years; however, advocates maintain that their English language proficiency in later years will be higher than if they had been in programs emphasizing an early transition. The Longitudinal Study was intended to provide multiyear data that could be used to evaluate such claims. Unfortunately, the reported data analyses included only single-year analyses. Thus, the major objectives of the study—to provide causal inferences to guide policy decisions and to evaluate the impact of different programs over multiple years—were not achieved. There were a number of methodological difficulties with the study design and data collection that contributed to the disappointing results of the study.

Study Design and Data Collection

The panel found much less documentation for the research design for the longitudinal phase than for the descriptive phase. The design document made available to the panel, "Overview of Research Design Plans," contained far less than was available for the descriptive phase. There was no comprehensive final report for the initial contract, which covered only design and data collection. As noted above, a separate contract for analyzing the data from the longitudinal phase was awarded to RTI, subcontractor for the data collection phase. The final report for the data analysis was written to describe analyses of the existing data (Burkheimer et al., 1989); there was no attempt to cover study design.

The sample of schools and school districts was a subsample of the original descriptive phase sample. First, the 36 school districts that received site visits in the descriptive study, had at least 200 LM-LEP students in either the first grade or third grades, and agreed to participate in the longitudinal phase were identified. Second, 25 of these 36 districts were chosen. The method by which the sample was reduced to 25 is not clear. An effort was made to include schools (1) that provided all five service clusters A through E (see Table 3–1); (2) with predominant language groups other than Spanish; and (3) in all major geographic regions in the United States.

Students in the sample consisted of six distinct groups. Two cohorts of students were followed: students entering first grade in the fall of 1985 (the first-grade cohort) and students entering third grade in the fall of 1985 (the third-grade cohort). Three different types of students were sampled in each cohort. The LEP group consisted of virtually all students in the respective cohort who were classified as limited-English proficient by local criteria. The English-proficient group consisted of those students not classified as LEP but who were receiving special services because they were placed in classes with LEP students. The comparison group consisted of children considered English proficient who had never been classified as LEP or received LEP services. Some sites had no comparison students, and the sampling of comparison students seems to have been very poorly controlled. Data from the study came from a total of 33 forms completed by students, parents, teachers, and school and district personnel over a period of 3 years. The documents made available to the panel provide no plans for data management or control of missing data, nor do they include the interviewer protocols.

Analysis Methods

Initial Plans

The data analyses actually performed bore little resemblance to the original plans. The research design plan called for two levels of analysis. First, "a single, national study" would be "based on the use of carefully chosen uniform measures to address a set of common research questions investigated across all participating schools." Second, "sets of linked mini-studies" would "address some questions of national interest which only apply in certain settings and to address questions of particular local interest to the participating school districts" (Development Associates, 1984a, page 5). The national studies were to include correlational analyses, including multiple and partial correlations. The researchers also planned to apply path analysis to derive causal associations between treatment variables and outcomes.

The initial contract for the Longitudinal Study did not cover data analysis. The funding for the subsequent data analysis contract was significantly scaled down from what had been originally planned. No linked ministudies were attempted. Hierarchical regression models were estimated, but as the authors noted, path-analytic interpretation of the parameters was unwarranted. Under the data analysis contract, a "Descriptive Report" produced some descriptive analyses of the longitudinal data and examined the feasibility of addressing the research objectives. A data analysis plan, which included a revised set of analysis questions (substantially reduced from the research questions), was then submitted. The analysis plan still proposed both estimation of structural parameters in path analysis models and multiyear analyses. Both of these objectives were dropped in the final data analyses.

Linked Ministudies   A major part of the original research plan for the Longitudinal Study was a series of linked ministudies. The research plan noted that many questions of major policy import could not be answered in a large national study, either because they concerned only some types of schools or programs or because they concerned variables which could not be directly combined across sites (such as, subjectively determined questionnaire responses whose interpretation might differ from site to site). The original research plan proposed that a set of linked ministudies be performed, with the results to be combined by meta-analysis (a set of statistical methods for combining the results of several studies). No detailed plans were presented for the linked ministudies. Which research questions were to be addressed by the single national study and which by the linked ministudies was not made clear. Only the single national study was performed. No mention of the linked ministudies was made in the data analysis plan or final report developed by RTI for the data analysis contract.

The panel concurs with the authors of the research plan overview that a set of linked ministudies is an appropriate methodology for assessing the effectiveness of different strategies for bilingual education. The research design and sampling plan of the longitudinal study were more appropriate, however, for a single national descriptive study than for a set of linked small-scale quasi-experiments. This point is discussed in more detail below.

Path Analysis   Path analysis is a statistical technique for estimating regression models in which there are several sets of equations relating predictor variables to predicted variables. In a path analysis model, a variable that is predicted in one equation may be a predictor variable in another. Variables in a path analysis model are organized into a directed graph referred to as a path diagram. Figure 3–1 shows a high-level path diagram taken from the research design plan of the Longitudinal Study. Path analysis models are also sometimes called "causal models" because the direction of the arrows in the path diagram is often taken to denote causality.

As an example, consider a simplified version of Figure 3–1 with two equations:

1. Instructional exposure (treatment) is modeled as a function of a set of background variables (covariates) plus a random error;
2. Achievement (outcome) is modeled as a function of the instructional exposure and background variables, plus a random error.

Statistical methods for estimating the parameters of path analysis models depend on certain assumptions about the relationships between the variables. (If these assumptions are not satisfied, the resulting estimates are inconsistent, meaning that even with very large sample sizes, the parameter estimates are not necessarily close to the actual parameter values.) These assumptions are described in Appendix B to the Overview of the Research Design Plans (Development Associates, 1984b).

In the example, the most important assumption is that the random prediction errors in the two equations are uncorrelated with the background variables. The authors of note (Development Associates, 1984b, Appendix B; italics in original):

> The rationale for this assumption is based upon the fact that the *important* variables are already included in the model and that the [prediction errors]

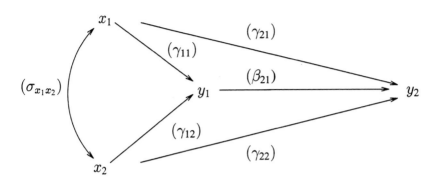

Hypothetical Model 1

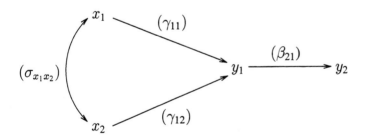

Hypothetical Model 2

FIGURE 3–1 Sample Path Diagrams from Research Plan

represent a composite of small random influences from a large number of sources (including measurement error) that can reasonably be expected to be independent of the major sources of influence.

If this assumption is met, then the first of the two equations can be estimated consistently with ordinary least squares regression. (Ordinary least squares regression is the most common regression estimation method and was used by RTI in the Longitudinal Study data analysis.) The second equation in the example uses the dependent variable from the first equation as one of the predictor variables. For this reason, a second assumption is required if ordinary least squares regression is to be used to estimate the parameters of this equation: namely that the random errors in the first and second equations are uncorrelated with each other. The research plan notes (Development Associates, 1984b, Appendix B) that:

> [this assumption] . . . is on less firm grounds than the assumption of independence between the [background variables] and the error terms. It may be unreasonable since some important variables may have been omitted from the model that may influence both [treatment] and [outcome].

(We note that this quote directly contradicts the previous quote from the same page of the Appendix, although the first is deemed plausible and the second implausible.)

The authors go on to describe statistical methods for estimating parameters of the equations when the second assumption (errors in equations 1 and 2 are uncorrelated) does not hold. They also describe approaches to estimating parameters when the variables are measured with error. Measurement error is one way in which the first assumption (errors are uncorrelated with predictor variables) can be violated. But the assumption remains that the errors in the regression equation relating the true values of the predictor and predicted variables (of which the observed values are "noisy" measurements) are uncorrelated with the true values of the predictor variables. This assumption would be violated if important variables were left out of the regression or if the regression model had the wrong functional form, invalidating any of the estimation approaches discussed in the research design plan.

When estimating any type of regression model, it is important to have sufficient independent variation among the important predictor variables. When predictor variables are highly correlated, parameter estimates are unstable. That is, large differences in parameter estimates make very little difference in how well the model fits the data. For example, if background variables are highly correlated with treatments, a model that includes only treatments and no background variables may be nearly indistinguishable in fit from a model that includes only background variables and no treatments. In other words, it is not possible to tell whether differences between treatment and control groups are due to the treatments or to the background variables. No statistical method, no matter how sophisticated, can make up for lack of adequate independent variation among treatments and background variables.

The common practice of dropping variables out of the model if leaving them in does not significantly improve model fit invalidates the assumptions under which parameters of a path analysis model can be consistently estimated, unless it can be argued that a parameter estimate that is not significantly different from zero really means that the variable has no or little effect. When there is insufficient independent variation among variables to reliably estimate model parameters, no such argument can be made. Therefore, dropping insignificant variables may invalidate the assumptions under which parameters can be consistently estimated.

Methodology Used

The primary data analysis method used in the Longitudinal Study was multiple regression analysis. The regression models are consistent with Figure 3–1. The final report states (Development Associates, 1984b, page 2–1) that "the sets of regression equations could be linked to define path analysis models," but the authors were careful to note that causal attribution is problematic. Nowhere else in the report is path analysis mentioned. All analyses in the final report were unweighted, and they were limited to the LEP group and to students whose native language was Spanish. Because of the extent of missing data, RTI attempted no multiyear analyses.

Estimates for four sets of linear regression models were included in the report:

- Receipt of services was modeled as a function of student and home background measures, ability/achievement measures, and educational history measures (Chapter 4).
- English language arts achievement was modeled as a function of instructional exposure measures, student and home background measures, ability/achievement measures, educational history measures, school/classroom measures, and measures of background characteristics and teaching style of the main language arts teacher (Chapter 5).
- Mathematics achievement was modeled as a function of instructional exposure measures, student and home background measures, ability/achievement measures, educational history measures, school/classroom measures, and measures of background characteristics and teaching style of the main mathematics teacher (Chapter 6).
- Exit of students from LEP services was modeled as a function of instructional exposure measures, student and home background measures, ability/achievement measures, educational history measures, school/classroom measures, and measures of background characteristics and teaching style of the main language arts teacher (Chapter 7).

These estimates were developed separately for each cohort and each year, but no achievement models were developed for the first year of the first-grade cohort because of the lack of pretest data.

The basic modeling approach can be summarized as follows. Modeling began with a set of "core" variables, which included the variables of major policy interest with respect to the variable being predicted. The remaining variables were divided into classes (such as school and district indicator variables, instructional exposure variables, educational history variables, ability/achievement variables, and various interactions among classes). The following four steps were used in modeling process:

1. Estimate a regression equation based on the "core" variables.
2. Add the next set of variables. Test whether the entire set of variables can be removed from the model without a significant decrease in explained variance.
3. If all new variables can be removed, do so. Otherwise, use stepwise backward elimination to remove variables from the added set.
4. Repeat steps 2 and 3 until no new sets of variables remain to be added.

Summary of Results

The final report for the longitudinal phase (Burkheimer et al., 1989) includes a summary of major study findings. In order for readers to fully appreciate the panel's concerns and critique, we present first the full report summary (emphases in original):

> Despite the considerable definitional and analytic constraints and the inconsistency of model solutions, a number of reasonably consistent and meaningful general conclusions relevant to the education of LEP children can be drawn from the findings. These conclusions are presented below.
>
> • **Assignment of LEP students to specific instructional service packages reflects principally local policy determinations. To a much smaller extent (and principally in the lower grades) assignment may be based on designed (and apparently criterion-driven) placement of students in the specific services for which they are ready.**
>
> Although the predictability of the instruction received by LEP children was highly variable (some types of instruction were highly predictable and others were not), the patterns of provided instruction seem to be set primarily at the school/district level and secondarily at the teacher/classroom level. Dummy variables, reflecting nothing more than membership in a cluster of schools/districts, generally contributed most of the explained variance in predicting the educational exposure variables. When combined with other school and classroom variables, which also served as clustering variables, these contextual factors accounted for (over-model median) over 93 percent of the explained variance in the instructional exposure variables.
>
> The findings also tended to indicate that instructional services were determined in part by the size of the LEP population being served within the district, school, or classroom. Patterns established at the level of these units may have been designated to meet the needs of the average child in the unit and, thus, may have subordinated other potential relationships between instructional exposure and home or individual child characteristics. Patterns of instruction received, when averaged over students within a study year, demonstrated systematic changes over the nominal grade placement levels associated with the study year. Indicators of relative English proficiency for

the individual LEP child played only a relatively small role in his/her receipt of particular instruction (for the variables examined here), principally in the earlier grades.

Deliberate assignment of LEP children to types of instruction consistent with explicit and implicit indicators of their greater proficiency in English was reflected in a weak trend (and probably occurred in many instances). However, an alternate explanation (which recognizes the implicit clustering of students within existing programs based on district policy) is considered equally plausible, particularly in light of the fact that oral English proficiency as measured in year 1 of the study was still predictive of services received in study year 3.

While not modeled directly, it seems quite reasonable (in light of the strong prediction obtained from school/district membership) that one of the best predictors of instructional exposure in any year is the type of instruction provided in the previous year (i.e., the nature of instructional exposure is principally a function of a consistent district policy, a supposition well supported in these analysis). In this case, if (as would certainly be expected) instruction in English language arts and in English generally facilitates English achievement (as measured in the short term), then the positive effect of prior year's instruction on the pretest for any given year, plus the continuity between the prior year's instruction and the current year's instruction, should have resulted in the types of relationships observed.

In actuality, it was probably the case that both of these hypothesized effects were in operation. Programs that used simplified English and oral English in previous years (recall that none of the models were addressed exclusively to students who had received no prior LEP services), toward developing transition to English as the language of instruction, should have realized some success in the achievement measures which would, in turn, have allowed greater use of standard English, less need for additional instruction in oral English, and a foundation on which to base increased instruction in English language arts and more instruction provided using English.

- **Too heavy a concentration on one specific aspect of the LEP child's education generally can detract from achievement in other areas.**

The effects of the instructional exposure variables in the models of mathematics and English language arts achievement were quite pronounced but rarely simple. In a number of cases, interactions among the instructional exposure variables indicated the trade-offs that are common to most education programs; namely, within a framework that constrains total instructional hours and is further constrained by legislated requirements for some courses, increased instruction in one particular subject area is typically accomplished at the expense of reduction in another subject area.

- **The yearly achievement of LEP students in mathematics and English language arts is not facilitated by a single approach; rather, different approaches seem more appropriate depending on the characteristics of the student. LEP students who are assigned to services for which they are ready generally show increased achievement (in both mathematics, as measured on an English test, and English language arts); however, if these services are provided before the child is ready such services may be counterproductive.**

Yearly achievement of LEP children was generally well predicted, and the nature of the instruction received by these children contributed substantially to explaining achievement. However, the large number of interactions between individual measures of prior proficiency and various measures of instruction indicated that the relationships were typically not simple ones. Findings indicated relatively consistently that greatest benefit from a particular combination of instructional strategies was realized by those who already possessed sufficient requisite skills. These same combinations of instructional services frequently resulted in lower net achievement when provided to LEP children who had not obtained the requisite proficiencies to benefit from the instruction; those children typically benefited from instructional services more attuned to the *different* skills that they possessed. Specific examples of these general conclusions are provided below.

- **When ready (i.e., with sufficiently high oral proficiency or prior achievement in English) and when provided more instruction in English language arts and/or indirect exposure to English through instruction provided in English in other courses, LEP children show greater yearly achievement in English language arts.**
- **When LEP children are weak in English and/or strong in their native language, English language arts instruction in the native language facilitates yearly English language arts achievement; to a lesser extent, mathematics instruction in the native language facilitates mathematics achievement under the same conditions.**
- **In earlier grades yearly mathematics achievement gains, as measured on a test in English, can be realized when mathematics instruction is provided principally in English *or* when the instruction is provided primarily in the native language. Achievement, in the former case, is facilitated by greater prior achievement on an English language math test; in the latter case, achievement is facilitated to the extent that the child receives more instruction in English language arts.**

  In later grades, regardless of the language in which the student learns mathematics, yearly achievement in mathematics, on an English language test, will not be realized until the child gains some mastery of English (through English language arts instruction or exposure to instruction in English in other courses, particularly mathematics).

Language of instruction in mathematics seems to play a considerably smaller role in the upper grades, however, it does continue to be reflected through the dummy variables in those less-powerful models. Consequently, if diverse instructional procedures (related to prior proficiencies, or lack thereof) prepare the children equally well, there should be no specific benefit associated with any specific approach. However, mathematics achievement in this study was measured through a test in the English language, and while at lower grade levels it is likely that much of the mathematics work may be language-free, such is not the case at upper grade levels where more direct effects are associated with higher English language proficiency. Thus, success on a test that is administered in English (be it a state-level competency test, a college placement test, or a job placement test) depends on acquisition of English language skills, regardless of the language in which the student has learned mathematics.

- **Like assignment to specific services, exit from LEP services reflects both local policy determinations (some of which are apparently independent of criteria measured by the analytic variables) and specific criterion-driven exit rules related to reaching certain levels of proficiency/achievement in English.**

The best predictor of exit was the school dummy variable set, which reflected little more than enrollment in specific clusters of schools and/or districts. This certainly reflects the fact that, under some conditions, retention in the LEP program was likely to be determined less by individual differences in English proficiency (particularly at the upper grade levels and during the later study years) than by district policy (which was probably determined, in part, by the size and nature of the LEP student population and the overall language-minority makeup of the general population within the district and/or school attendance area). Also, the contributions from other variables were generally attributable to how those variables clustered together at a school or district level (that were not adequately captured by the dummy variables).

Thus, the prime determinations of exiting at upper grade levels appear to be school or district policies relating to the entire remaining group (or at least the greater portion of it) of students being served. At the lower grade levels even with the mixed policies of criterion and non-criterion retention in services, relationships existed between exit and individual factors, exposure to specific instruction, and enhanced achievement in English language arts (probably as a result of that exposure). Nonetheless, these effects were also modified by school characteristics (clustered within districts), such that the relationships existed (or were most pronounced) only in certain types of schools. It seems quite likely that the characteristics of those schools were related to the programs that were using specific criteria for retention in services rather than programs that were retaining all (or nearly all) LEP students in those grades.

Exit rate patterns themselves were indicative of the nature of exit from LEP services over time (or grade). The conditional exit rates (i.e., rate of exit for those who had not exited previously) in both cohorts were greatest in the first two years of the study. Analyzed within the different school districts, the data showed markedly different lower-bound cumulative exit rates and over-year patterns. Some districts had exited virtually all of their LEP students prior to nominal Grade 5, while others had exited essentially none. Some districts showed a steady increase in exit rate over the years and others showed early exit of a subgroup of LEP students, with little subsequent increment. This suggests that some programs were retaining children in LEP services on the basis of some criterion that increased over subsequent years (i.e., perhaps achievement in English language arts), while others were maintaining services to all or a subgroup of LEP students irrespective of external criteria.

- **Children receiving patterns of services that also enhance English language arts achievement, and/or patterns more similar to those that would be expected for English-proficient children, are more likely to be exited from LEP services.**

One relatively consistent finding for exit was exhibited in one way or another in all of the models; namely, during a given year, children who were receiving services more akin to those that would be provided to English-proficient students were more likely to be exited, while those who were not were less likely to be exited. Also, in a number of instances, interactive patterns that predicted exit were quite similar to the patterns that had been found to predict achievement gains in English language arts. Greater prior achievement in English language arts and/or initial oral proficiency in English (typically as modified by certain combinations of instructional services) were also found to increase the probability of exit for children in all but the least powerful of the models (i.e., in the later grades).

To the extent that retention in the LEP program was based on individual student needs, the higher achievers would be exited from the program. This did happen to a small extent (note also that achievement variables did show up in some main effects and in a relatively small number of interactions); however, the effects from these variables were not nearly as strong or numerous as would be expected if individual achievement were being consistently considered in exit decisions. This indicates that decisions regarding both the type of instruction (resulting in differences in English proficiency/achievement) and the policy for exiting were probably made more on a school or district level for all (or major groups of) students than for individual students based on their level of proficiency in English. This may reflect either a deliberate placement of students in "pre-exit" conditions or the use of those specific patterns in programs that have managed to increase achievement in prior years and provide these particular combinations of services in the year of exit.

The relationships of exit to instruction similar to that provided to English-proficient students (and conversely non-exit to services more directed to LEP students) also seems to reflect a sound educational practice. Children who are in small classes and for whom there is considerable use of simple English in instruction (both of which were associated with reduced probability of exit) are probably in such an instructional environment because they need special attention; as such, the students are not likely candidates for exit from service during the year. Similarly, children receiving instruction in oral English (associated with reduction in probability of exit) probably need such instruction because of a lack of English proficiency, and consequently would be kept in the LEP program for one or more additional years.

It is conceivable that students who had the greatest need for continuation of LEP services were grouped into individual classrooms (where a large number of options for educational services were viable), while those less in need (and nearing the point where they could be exited) were placed in classrooms with larger proportions of English-proficient students. It is considered more likely, however, that districts or schools with high proportions of LEP students (which would certainly lead to large proportions of LEP students in *all* classrooms) had a larger number of viable options for provision of services to their LEP populations, including longer-term programatic efforts, with policies that would probably favor retention in the LEP program at the higher grade/age levels.

These reported conclusions are based on dubious statistical methodology (see "Critical Review of Longitudinal Phase Study," below). Although the author note the problems with drawing defensible causal inferences from these data, these difficulties are not reflected in the way these conclusions are worded. For example, the report states (Burkheimer et al., 1989; italics added):

> When LEP children are weak in English and/or strong in their native language, English language arts instruction in the native language *facilitates* yearly English language arts achievement; to a lesser extent, mathematics instruction in the native language *facilitates* mathematics achievement under the same conditions.

What can defensibly be said is that a positive partial correlation was observed between achievement and the respective instructional variable when the effects of other variables in the model were taken into account. Such a correlation may be *suggestive* of a positive causal connection, but the panel notes that due to many problems with the data and analyses, none of the report's conclusions can be regarded as verified by these data.

We note, however, that some of the report's conclusions are consistent with other findings in the literature, including conclusions from the Immersion Study. The panel has noted that when several studies carried out under different conditions yield convergent results, confidence in the conclusions increases, even if the individual studies are flawed. The panel still urges caution in combining (flawed) studies, particularly if the flaws are much the same from study to study.

Critical Review of Longitudinal Phase Study

Study Design

A major objective of the descriptive phase of the Longitudinal Study was to provide information relevant to the design of the longitudinal phase. The longitudinal phase reused the sample taken for the descriptive phase, benefited from the descriptive phase experience with similar types of data collection instruments and methods, and made use of relationships established with school personnel. It appears, however, that the *results* of the descriptive phase had little influence on the design of the longitudinal phase..

This is unfortunate because the Descriptive Phase Report reveals a number of warning signs that should have signaled potential problems during the longitudinal phase. The study timeline (see "The Descriptive Phase," above) suggests why these warning signs may not have been heeded. Data collection for the descriptive phase occurred in the fall of 1983. The research design plan for the longitudinal phase was submitted in the spring of 1983, but the Descriptive Phase Report was not submitted until December of 1984, after the baseline data for the longitudinal phase had been collected. To meet this schedule, an initial sampling design and drafts of data collection instruments would have had to have been prepared well in advance of spring 1983 when plans were submitted. It appears that the broad framework of the longitudinal phase design was settled before any results from the descriptive study were available. The tight time schedule prevented the results of the descriptive phase from having a major impact on the sample design and data collection, even though they suggest that major changes were needed. More specific criticisms of the study design are considered below.

Study Objectives   A successful observational study must have clearly defined objectives, and these objectives must be ranked to reflect some form of priority. As became clear during implementation, the original objectives of the study were far too ambitious, and not all objectives could be realized. Resource restrictions always require tradeoffs among objectives, and dropping infeasible or low-priority objectives early in a study enables resources to be concentrated on ensuring that high-priority objectives will be met.

To illustrate this point, consider the descriptive phase results that revealed that a large majority of LM-LEP students were Spanish speaking, that these students differed in many important ways from other LM-LEP students, and that there was a strong relationship between native language and service characteristics. Within available resources under the existing sampling plan, there was little hope that the sample would contain sufficient numbers of students with sufficient variation in treatments to make reliable inferences relating native language to all other variables of interest. Aggregating across language groups was problematic because of known differences between the populations. A strong case could have been made *a priori* for limiting the study to Spanish-speaking LM-LEP students and dropping the objectives relating to language groups other than Spanish. Doing this at the outset (rather than having it forced after the fact due to the inevitable data problems) might have made resources available for better control of missing data. This in turn might have enabled a longitudinal analysis, albeit limited to Spanish-speaking students.

Definition of the Unit of Inference   For most analyses, the researchers attempted to use students as the unit of inference. The rationale for this was that different students in the same school or classroom might receive different treatments, and the researchers wanted to be able to analyze the effect of these differences. There was a strong correlation, however, between services provided to different students in the same classroom, school, or district. In many cases, the instructional variables were highly confounded with school and district indicator variables because certain types of instructional practices were clustered within certain schools or districts. This confounding severely limited the power of the analysis and the ability to distinguish between effects of treatments and effects of highly correlated covariates. Yet this clustering could have been anticipated from the information available from the descriptive phase.

When there is a high degree of clustering, a large sample of *students* does not guarantee high precision in the results. Of more importance to precision is the number of *schools* or *districts*, which was not large (118 schools in 25 districts).

Definition of the Subject Population   The contractors decided at the outset of the study to use local definitions to classify students as LEP. Therefore, the definition of who was eligible for inclusion in the analysis varied from school to school. As noted above, in some cases LEP classification may have had more to do with availability of funds or school/district policy for length of stay in LEP programs than with English-language proficiency. Thus, important characteristics of the subject pool (including unmeasured characteristics) appear to be confounded with school and district variables. In addition, the definition of LEP, and thus the definition of the target population, may differ from year to year. Because treatments tended to cluster within schools and districts, it is likely that important characteristics of the subject pool are confounded with assignment to treatments. This problem could have been anticipated from the descriptive phase results, which indicated that both LEP classification and service features depended on school and district policy and varied widely among districts.

Treatment Definition   The Department of Education was interested in the impact of a number of instructional variables on English acquisition. Development Associates (1984b) identified 10 different categories of "treatment variables" planned to be used in causal modeling. A number of these treatment variables were subcategorized into three or four distinct variables. The descriptive phase had identified five distinct service clusters, and the original research questions (see below) concerned the effects of these clusters on achievement.

Unlike the situation in an experiment however, there was substantial variation in how treatments were applied within the service clusters. The service clusters were not used in the final data analyses; models were built using the treatment variables directly. Of course, the existence of clusters in the population restricted the range of independent variation of treatments, thus restricting the inferences that could be made about distinct effects. (For example, use of the native language in mathematics instruction tended to correlate with use of the native language in language arts instruction because both tended to occur more in programs emphasizing a gradual transition to English; therefore, inferences about separate influences of these variables are problematic.)

Because there is no well-defined protocol for treatments, it may be impossible to separate genuine treatment effects from the effects of covariates that affect how treatments are actually applied. For example, when use of the native language is emphasized, teachers tend to have higher native-language proficiency and lower English proficiency than when English is emphasized; teachers with credentials in LM-LEP education tend to cluster in programs emphasizing slower transition to English. These effects must be considered to be part of the treatments as actually administered. It is important to stress that conclusions apply only to treatments *as administered in a study*, and not necessarily to proposed treatments in which the values of important covariates differ from those observed in the study. That is, conclusions about the effects of programs emphasizing slower transition to English would not apply if they were taught by teachers with low Spanish proficiency.

There does not appear to have been any *a priori* attempt to analyze the range of variation in treatments and assess whether there was sufficient variation to address the study objectives.

Covariates and Outcomes   The distinction between covariates and outcomes is not appropriately addressed in the Longitudinal Study. Outcomes (for example, test scores) at one time period are used as covariates for analyses of the data for the next time period. There were no true pretests for the study. All test scores were obtained from students who had been receiving one or another treatment prior to the beginning of the study.

Selection of Units into the Sample   The sample of schools for the longitudinal phase consisted of those schools from the descriptive phase sample with a sufficient number of LM-LEP students. The two phases had different purposes, and different sample selection criteria were appropriate. In the descriptive phase, the concern was with coverage—ensuring that the sample represented the wide range of treatments in the population. For drawing causal inferences it is essential to control for the effects of variables other than the putative causal factors. The major concern should be comparability of units in the different treatment categories. There is no reason to expect a sample selected for coverage to show the required comparability.

The descriptive phase concern for coverage carried over, inappropriately, to the longitudinal phase. The selection criteria attempted to ensure coverage of a wide range of treatments and language groups, with little concern for whether the sample would contain enough observations to make reliable inferences. For example, the research design plan, in describing how the 25 school districts were chosen from the qualifying 36 districts, states that "an effort was made to assure inclusion of clusters A, D and E." Three schools in the final sample had service cluster E. There was no discussion of whether this was sufficient for reliable statistical inference, nor was there any analysis of the comparability of these three schools to schools offering other treatments. The plan stated that some schools offered multiple treatments, but it did not state whether the three E-cluster schools also offered other treatments.

To determine whether one of two treatment types is more effective, the sample would have needed to contain districts or schools that are similar in important respects (e.g., policy towards classifying LM-LEP students, student characteristics, and teacher characteristics) with the exception of treatment type. Differences in outcomes might then be attributed to differences in treatment type and not to differences in those other variables. The descriptive phase sample contained information on many variables pertaining to characteristics of students, teachers, and treatments. It also provided information on LM-LEP classification policy. It would thus have been possible to analyze the descriptive phase sample to determine which causal inferences were and were not possible for that sample. Those objectives that could not be met from the existing sample could then have been made a priority. If judged cost-beneficial, the sample could have been augmented by selecting additional schools covering the range of variation needed to make inferences on high-priority objectives.

These concerns were recognized in the planning documents (Development

Associates, 1984b). The impossibility of assigning subjects randomly to treatments was noted, and the issue of controlling for biases was discussed. Standard methods of adjusting for potential biases include matching or subclassification on the basis of covariates and/or model-based adjustment. These methods were discussed in a general way in the planning documents; however, specific procedures were not defined. There appears to have been no planning to control for the effect of potential hidden biases or effects due to unmeasured covariates. The report recognized that data were extremely poor or unavailable for some potentially important covariates, but there appear to have been no plans for anything other than qualitative assessment of the effects of those data. No consideration appears to have been given to augmenting the sample to ensure the necessary variability even though data available from the descriptive phase could have identified problems of insufficient variation in treatments and noncomparability of units.

Determination of Sample Size Required for Reliable Inferences Having a large overall sample is not sufficient for drawing conclusions when the goal is to infer relationships among variables. There are two aspects that need to be carefully considered in any study. One is the level of significance of a result, or, roughly speaking, the likelihood that a seemingly significant outcome has occurred by chance alone. The second aspect is the power of the study, or the likelihood that the study will be able to detect an effect of a given size. Power analyses need to be performed for specific analyses of major importance, and these power analyses must take into account not just the raw numbers of observations, but the number of observations expected to exhibit specific patterns of covariates. For example, if service clusters are highly correlated with variables thought to influence outcomes of interest (for example, a particular service cluster occurs only in districts dominated by students of low socioeconomic status), then estimating effects due to treatment alone will be virtually impossible. In experiments, treatments are generally randomized within cells defined by covariates in order to ensure sufficient independent variation of treatments and covariates. This approach is not possible in an observational study. When initial data, such as that from the descriptive study, are available, it is often possible to determine ahead of time whether sufficient variation exists within the population to make the desired inferences. If not, resources can be concentrated on collecting the data required for analyses that are more likely to be fruitful, or the sample can be augmented with additional schools chosen specifically to obtain combinations of treatments and covariates not represented in the initial sample.

Data Collection

Failure to Control for Missing Data Missing data can undermine attempts to derive any inferences from statistical data, but missing data are particularly problematic when causal inferences are contemplated. Missing data rates that are quite acceptable for estimating the mean and variance of a single variable can undermine the determination of relationships between several variables. For relational analysis, *patterns* of missing data are more important than raw rates of missing data. Longitudinal studies also compound problems of missing data. Without careful planning for the control of missing data, missing data is likely to undermine a longitudinal study involving relational analysis.

Concerns about missing data are especially acute for the Longitudinal Study. This could have been anticipated. Data from the study came from a total of 33 forms completed by students, parents, teachers, and school and district personnel over a period of 3 years. Many of these forms were quite complicated. The research design plan called for more than 50 variables to be involved in causal modeling.

A simple calculation reveals the pitfalls awaiting unwary investigators. If 50 variables each have a 98 percent completion rate, and completion rates are independent between questions, then only 36 percent of the cases would be expected to have complete data for a single year. If completion rates are also independent across years, the completion rate over 3 years is about 5 percent. Of course, completion rates in the study were not independent between questions; however, missing data rates were much higher than 2 percent. In fact, even after preliminary imputation and the dropping of some variables from the analysis, fewer than 3 percent of the cases in either cohort had complete data required for analyses over all 3 years (Burkheimer et al., 1989). It was for this reason that the plan for multiyear analyses was abandoned.

It is essential to plan a strategy for minimizing and controlling for the effects of missing data. It does not appear that this was done in the Longitudinal Study. The term "missing data" was mentioned only once in the Overview of Research Design Plans (Development Associates, 1984b, Appendix B): "Among the potential data anomalies ... the most obvious is that of missing data, which can have serious implications for subsequent modeling." This observation was not followed up with any plans for coping with missing data. Unit nonresponse rates were reported for the descriptive phase and in the year 1 report of the longitudinal phase. No item nonresponse rates were reported, much less analyses of patterns of missing items. The planning documents contained no strategy for control or monitoring of missing data. Missing data problems can be mitigated with proper planning and proper monitoring. Problems can be identified early so that resources can be redirected away from collecting data that will turn out to be useless (see below).

High Levels of Attrition   Sample sizes were dramatically reduced from year to year, both because of students' exit from LEP programs and because of the mobility of the LM-LEP population. Plans called for follow-up of students who moved away, but student mobility turned out to be even greater than had been expected (study students transferred to over 500 nonstudy schools.) The magnitude of the data collection effort precluded follow-up, except for students who stayed within study districts. This problem could not have been anticipated from the single-year descriptive sample.

Sample shrinkage due to exit implies that the nature of the population of

LM-LEP students changed from year to year. Moreover, differential exit policies means that the nature of the population change differed from program to program. This difficulty was anticipated, which was a major reason given for attempting to follow exiting students.

Measurement Error   The descriptive phase report contains little information about the quality of the data. Inconsistencies among data items suggests that there was considerable measurement error for many variables. To the extent that the study instruments and data collection methods were similar, measurement error problems should have been similar. The descriptive phase thus should have provided information about the necessity of applying methods for controlling or adjusting for measurement error. In view of the important effect of measurement error on the ability to estimate parameters of interest in path analysis models, the lack of attention devoted to planning for and controlling measurement error is a serious omission.

Unmeasured Covariates   Constructs of great importance were never measured or measured very poorly. For example, pretest data were not collected for the first-grade cohort, nor for some students in the third-grade cohort. Measures of prior exposure to LEP services were very weak, limiting the inferences that could be drawn from the sample.

Changes in Forms   The final report for the data analysis contract states that changes were made in forms from year to year in order to "improve" them. This is contrary to sound statistical practice. Consistency in the meaning of data items from year to year is essential to a reliable longitudinal analysis.

Data Analysis Methods

The statistical analysis in the Longitudinal Study focused exclusively on regression and correlational analysis. The modeling proceeded by adding batches of variables to a regression model and then successively eliminating variables that did not significantly improve model fit. The modeling was not based on *a priori* theoretical considerations, except that candidate variables were chosen because it was thought they might affect outcomes of interest.

The data exhibited a high degree of multicollinearity: that is, many of the explanatory variables were themselves highly correlated with each other. As a result of this multicollinearity, many different models might have fit nearly as well as the ones reported. This was noted in the report. The report also noted that certain results, especially counterintuitive ones or ones that exhibited inconsistency from year to year, should be interpreted with caution. In particular, it is not generally accurate to say that a measured quantity (variable) that does not appear in a model has, as the report states, "no effect." The variable may well be related to the outcome being predicted by the model, but provide no incremental prediction effect because it is correlated with a variable that does appear in the model. Conversely, a variable that does appear in the model may be no better a pbredictor than some correlated variable that does not appear in the model.

It should also be noted that any reported significance levels need be viewed with suspicion when the modeling proceeded by trying a number of models and selecting the best; see, for example, Miller (1981). The report also notes the high degree of multicollinearity among the predictor variables. This multicollinearity further obfuscates the conclusions that can be drawn because the predictive power of one variable may be completely masked by other variables. Thus, a nonsignificant coefficient may imply that the corresponding variable has limited impact on predictions or that other correlated variables have masked the effect. The data analysis reported in the study must be more nearly viewed as an exploratory analysis than a theoretically driven *quasi-experiment* (see Chapter 2). Although the initial intent was a quasi-experiment, the study was not planned or executed in a way that enabled more than exploratory analyses. Exploratory analyses can serve the important purpose of suggesting hypotheses for later verification, however, firmly grounded causal inferences require carefully thought-out, planned, and executed experiments or quasi-experiments.

FURTHER ANALYSES

Despite the above criticisms, there may still be value to be gleaned from the data, albeit not to answer the intended questions. The panel found that the data provide a picture of the state of bilingual education in the early to mid-1980s and might be useful in planning further studies.

Descriptive Phase Data

The descriptive phase of the Longitudinal Study presents a large set of data that can be reliably projected to the national population of (locally defined) LM-LEP students, or a large majority of it, without substantial problems of bias or imprecision. As such, it is a useful resource for researchers attempting to understand the range of services being provided to LM-LEP students and a valuable knowledge base for use in planning studies of the effectiveness of programs.

One of the inherent difficulties with the Longitudinal Study (and the Immersion Study) is the difficulty of correctly classifying LM-LEP service programs, and indeed of even finding good examples of any given type. One possibly useful application of the descriptive phase data would be a more detailed characterization of the types of services offered and the characteristics of the students to whom they were offered. This work might concentrate future evaluation efforts on those types of programs currently widely offered and to cover the full range of such programs. Information might also be extracted about the extent to which specific types of services are targeted to student needs and capabilities, rather than being a function of the resources available to the school. Such analyses could view service delivery as a multidimensional phenomenon, considering the interrelationships exhibited among the five variables used to define service clusters, plus possibly others. Such analyses have the potential to shed substantial light as to what is actually "out there" and, just as importantly, why. This could well serve future debates and investigations about the efficacies of different programs.

Yet one caveat must be noted. The data from the descriptive study were collected in 1983. No doubt the population of LM-LEP students has changed substantially since then. The nature and range of services offered has probably also changed. Hence, results from any further analyses of these data would necessarily be dated.

Longitudinal Phase Data

Descriptive Analyses of Year 1 Data   The baseline data for the longitudinal analyses were collected during 1984–1985. The data were collected about districts, schools, teachers, classrooms, and students from a subset of those schools and districts surveyed during the descriptive phase with sufficient LM-LEP students to make the Longitudinal Study data collection effort cost effective. Some schools declined to participate, and for some of these substitutions were made, but no weighting adjustments were made to reflect this nonresponse. All LEP students and English-proficient students receiving LEP services in grades 1 and 3 were included, plus a sample of students who had never been LEP or received services (comparison students). Survey weights were not developed for the data. The sampling procedures for selecting the comparison students were so poorly controlled that weighting of these students within schools was not possible even if it had been deemed desirable.

The Descriptive Report of the Longitudinal Study (Development Associates, 1984a) provides details of the variables collected in the longitudinal phase. The process of arriving at derived variables is described and limitations of the data, particularly the extent of missing data problems, are described.

Given the large volume of baseline data collected, the question arises as to whether there are useful descriptive analyses of these data that have not been undertaken thus far, but that might be done and might shed light on the delivery of services to LM-LEP students. Some issues related to this question are addressed in this section.

In general, there were considerable problems with missing and unreliable data. Many of these are discussed in some detail in the descriptive report. These problems appear to have been so severe that, if any finding derived from them contradicted the "conventional wisdom" about bilingual education, the finding could easily be dismissed as an artifact of the poor data. There may, however, be components of the data that are worthy of additional analyses.

Any generalization of descriptive analyses from sample to target population would be on much firmer ground if the analyses incorporated survey weights. The panel does concur with the investigator in concluding that it is unlikely that useful survey weights could be developed for the longitudinal sample.

In the descriptive phase, 342 schools were identified as having sufficient LM-LEP students for the study, yet only 86 schools participated in the longitudinal phase. This implies that a more restrictive population was used than is made clear in the description on page 2 (Development Associates, 1984a). The report does not make it clear how the reduction to 86 schools was accomplished. Furthermore, the participation of only 86 schools from a smaller number of districts means that the level of sampling error is likely to be moderately high, despite the inclusion of several thousand students in the sample.

The variables that appear to be most complete, and also numerous, are the school-level variables derived from teacher data and the teacher-level variables. The three derived classroom-level variables, classroom size, percentage of students who are LEP, and the percentage of students who speak only English, also appear to be relatively free from missing data and measurement error problems. One important use for these data might be to cross classify these school-, teacher- and classroom-level variables, perhaps weighted by the numbers of LEP students in the classroom, in order to characterize the type of learning environments that LM-LEP students are exposed to (or were in 1984–1985). For example, simple cross-classification of "Teacher support for using child's native language in teaching him/her" (the variable coded as SCLM1Y1 in the report) with "Principal support of school's LM-LEP program" (coded as SCLM4Y1) might provide information about the distribution of teacher support for native language usage and its association with a principal's support for LM-LEP programs. This in turn might shed some light on the relationship of school policies to teacher practices. Cross-classification of some of the teacher characteristic variables with the percentage of students in a class that are LEP (coded as CLSPLEP1) would provide information not only about the distributions of different teaching practices for LM-LEP students, and the variations in the percentage of students who are LM-LEP (in this "high LEP" population), but might also be informative about whether certain types of teacher services and practices are predominantly available in classrooms with mostly LEP students, or in those with few LEP students.

In summary, it is unclear from the Descriptive Report how restricted the population for inference is from the longitudinal phase. This must be addressed before a conclusion can be reached as to whether further descriptive analyses are warranted. There do appear to be a substantial number of reliable variables that could be analyzed, and in particular cross-classified, with a view to better characterizing the range of learning environments to which LM-LEP students are exposed and their relative prevalence in practice. Such analyses might guide future efforts at evaluating programs, at least by identifying what "programs" actually exist from the viewpoint of a LM-LEP elementary school student.

Other Analyses   It is possible that some defensible causal inferences could be drawn from the Longitudinal Study; however, it would take considerable effort just to determine the feasibility of such analyses.

The value of purely exploratory analyses might be enhanced after additional exploration of the robustness of the findings and the degree to which alternate models fit the data. Variables not appearing in a model but highly correlated with model variables might be substituted to evaluate whether an alternate model based on these variables would fit as well. For example, school-level, classroom-level, and teacher-level variables might be substituted for the school and district indicator variables.

Cross-validation might improve confidence in the robustness of the results. The models would be extremely suspect if coefficients changed drastically when the model was fit on a subset of the data, especially if the resulting models were poor predictors of the hold-out samples. No such analyses were performed as part of the original study, but they might be desirable given the degree of multicollinearity and other problems.

Finally, no attempt was made to analyze data from students who exited LEP programs, English-proficient students, or students whose native language was not Spanish. It is likely that sample sizes are too small for the latter two categories, but exploratory analyses for students who exited, of the type already performed for LEP students, may be of interest.

PROSPECTS FOR THE FUTURE

General Remarks

Contrary to the hopes of those who commissioned the Longitudinal Study, further research is needed to address the question of which interventions are most effective in improving educational outcomes for LM-LEP children. Despite all its problems the study does provide a valuable information base for designing future studies to address these objectives. The descriptive phase study provides information concerning the natural range of variation in services in the population and about correlations between service types and various background characteristics. The longitudinal phase adds to this information base: variables were measured in the longitudinal phase that were not in the descriptive phase, measurements were made over time, and information was collected about the factors related to exit from LM-LEP services. Although they must be regarded as exploratory in nature, the longitudinal phase analyses revealed associations between variables. Hypotheses about the causal mechanisms underlying these associations could be confirmed by well-designed and carefully implemented quasi-experimental studies.

Just as important, the study provides important information about the difficulties awaiting future researchers. The measurement difficulties, missing data problems, and attrition problems encountered by the Longitudinal Study will have to be faced by future researchers. Awareness of the magnitude of the problems permits planning to mitigate their impacts.

Planning for Observational Studies Directed to Causal Inference

At least seven factors must be attended to in planning an observational study if it is to be used for policy-relevant questions of causation.

First a successful observational study must have clearly defined study objectives, and these objectives must be made a priority. Resource restrictions always require tradeoffs between objectives. Dropping infeasible or low-priority objectives early in a study enables resources to be concentrated on ensuring that high-priority objectives will be met. Too many objectives without clear priorities often leads to failure to achieve any objectives.

Second, a clear, operational definition of treatments is essential and that means a full characterization of treatments as implemented.

Third, after the treatments have been designed, a sampling plan must be developed that ensures that comparable subjects are assigned to each of the treatments. Collecting data on covariates with the hope of adjusting or matching after the fact invites problems unless there is some assurance that the treatment groups will be reasonably comparable with respect to the distribution of covariates. A safer approach is to select observational units that are explicitly matched on key covariates. This approach requires data on which to base selection of matched units. The knowledge base gained from the Longitudinal Study, if used properly, can provide an extremely valuable resource for sample selection for future studies.

Fourth, there must be control of missing data. Missing data can undermine attempts to derive causal inferences from statistical data. It is essential to plan a strategy for minimizing and controlling for the effects of missing data. This issue is discussed in detail in the next section. Here, we note the critical importance of identifying key data items for which it is essential to have complete data, monitoring the completeness of these items as the survey progresses, and devoting resources to follow-up on these items if the extent of missing data becomes too high.

Fifth, there must be control of measurement error. If a model is defined at the outset with clearly specified hypotheses, it is possible to identify a priori the variables for which measurement error could seriously affect results. Special attempts might be made to measure these variables accurately or estimate a statistical model for the measurement error distribution. Information about key variables can be obtained from multiple sources (for example, school records and interviews). Multiple questions can be asked about the same variable and responses checked for consistency. A small subsample might be selected for intensive efforts to determine these variables accurately; a measurement error model might then be estimated by comparing the accurately assessed values for these cases with their initial error-prone responses.

Sixth, planning must include determination of the sample size required for reliable inferences. Having a large sample is not sufficient when the goal of a study is to infer relationships among variables. Power analyses need to be performed for specific analyses of major importance, and these power analyses must take into account not just the raw numbers of observations, but the observations expected to exhibit specific patterns of covariates. If, for example, service clusters are highly correlated with variables thought to influence outcomes of interest (for example, a particular service cluster occurs only in districts dominated by students of low socioeconomic status), then estimating effects due to treatment alone will be impossible. In experiments, treatments are generally randomized within cells defined by covariates in order to assure sufficient independent variation of treatments and covariates. This is not possible in an observational study; however, especially when initial data such as that from the Longitudinal Study are available, it may be possible to determine ahead of time whether sufficient variation exists within the population to make the desired inferences. If not, resources can be concentrated on collecting data required for analyses that are more likely to be fruitful. In determining a sample size it is again crucial to consider the issue of the appropriate unit of inference. Sample size calculations must also address missing data and, in a longitudinal study, expected attrition of sample units. Results of such analysis can be used to guide resource tradeoffs.

Finally, there must be careful monitoring of survey execution. As data are collected and coded, counts should be maintained of missing data, and preliminary correlational analyses can be run to determine whether the sample is showing sufficient variation among key variables. Adjustments can be made to correct for problems as they are identified. In some cases, it may turn out that some objectives cannot be met; resources can then be redirected to ensure the satisfaction of other important objectives.

Strategies for Control of Missing Data

Missing data problems can be greatly reduced (although seldom eliminated entirely) by proper planning and execution of a data collection effort.

A National Research Council report (Madow, Nisselson, and Olkin, 1983) states: "Almost every survey should be planned assuming nonresponse will occur, and at least informed guesses about nonresponse rates and biases based on previous experience and speculation should be made." Among the steps that can be taken to reduce nonresponse or its impact on results are the following (see Madow, Nisselson, and Olkin (1983) for a more complete set of recommendations):

- Based on study goals, identify a set of key variables for which it is essential to have relatively complete data.
- Collect data as completely and accurately as possible, using follow-ups and callbacks as necessary. A final follow-up using supervisors and superior interviewers may be necessary. Consider using a shorter and/or simpler questionnaire for the final follow-up. Pay special attention to key data items.
- Monitor data completeness as the study progresses; make adjustments in the data collection strategy as necessary to respond to the actual pattern of missing data.
- Plan strategies for collecting data items anticipated to be especially difficult to collect. Adjust strategies as data collection progresses.
- Monitor completion rates by important classifications of covariates. (This recommendation is crucial if relational analysis is the goal).

- Avoid unnecessarily complex and time-consuming questionnaires. Design questions to be nonthreatening and easy to understand.
- Consider including questions that are useful for modeling and adjusting for nonresponse. Consider including simpler or less-threatening versions of questions for which high non-response rates are anticipated (notice that this recommendation conflicts with the prior one; obviously a tradeoff is required).
- Make sure that the sample size is sufficiently large to compensate for missing data.
- To the extent possible, describe and/or model the missing data process and the degree to which respondents differ from non-respondents.
- Attempt to select cells for imputation so that respondents and non-respondents are as similar as possible within cells.
- If possible, use multiple imputation to improve estimates and estimates of variances. Explore the effects of alternate assumptions regarding the response process.
- Discuss and/or model biases that are the result of missing data.

LONGITUDINAL STUDY RESEARCH QUESTIONS

Reprinted here are the revised set of research objectives for the Longitudinal Study. This material is quoted verbatim from Exhibit 2 of the Longitudinal Report (Development Associates, 1984b):

A. What are the effects of the special services provided for LM/LEP students in grades 1–6?

    1. Effects of specific student characteristics

        a. Comprehension of native language (oral & written)

            1) What is the relationship between LM/LEP student's oral proficiency in the native language and the learning of English?

            2) How is a LM/LEP student's oral proficiency in the native language related to the learning of English when the student's native language is:

                a) A language linguistically related to English?
                b) A language linguistically distant from English?

            3) What is the relationship between a LM/LEP student's literacy in the native language and the acquisition of literacy in English when the native language is a language linguistically related to English (e.g. Spanish, Portuguese)? When it is not related?

            4) What is the relationship between a student's general ability and native language proficiency?

        b. Classroom behavior
        What is the relationship between LM/LEP students' classroom behaviors and success in school?

        c. Parents' interest and involvement

What is the relationship between LM/LEP parents' interest and involvement in their child's education and the child's success in school?

2. Effect of extent or duration of services

   a. What are the effects of length or duration of receipt of special services on the subsequent achievement of LM/LEP students?

   b. How do LM/LEP students who are receiving or have received special services for LM/LEP students compare with LM/LEP students who have never received such services?

3. Effects of site (classroom, school, or district) and staff characteristics

   a. What is the effect of linguistic isolation; e.g., being in a school where few or no students speak the same language, on the time required to learn English?

   b. To what extent does the degree of teacher and staff familiarity with the native culture of the LM/LEP students affect student achievement.

   c. To what extent does the educational background of teacher and staff affect the achievement of LM/LEP students?

4. Effects of conditions for exiting

   a. To what extent is oral proficiency in English correlated with proficiency in handling the written language (e.g., reading comprehension) and with academic achievement?

   b. When students are exited from special services after a fixed time, without regard to level of performance on some criterion variable, what is the effect on the student's subsequent achievement?

B. How do the various combinations of special services, or "service clusters," provided for LM/LEP students in grades 1–6 compare in terms of the effectiveness with which recipients subsequently can function in all English medium classrooms? (A service cluster is a set of instructional services provided to a particular student at a particular point in time).

   1. Effects by specific student characteristics

      a. Socioeconomic status

         1) Which clusters work best with LM/LEP students whose socioeconomic status is low?

         2) Which clusters work best with LM/LEP students whose socioeconomic status is middle or high?

      b. General academic ability

         1) Which clusters work best for LM/LEP children whose ability level is high?

         2) Which clusters work best for LM/LEP children whose ability level is low?

      c. English proficiency

         1) Which clusters are most effective for children who speak little or no English?

         2) Which clusters are most effective for children who speak some English, but nonetheless, cannot benefit from a mainstream classroom?

      d. Grade level
         Which clusters are most effective for LM/LEPs by grades?

    e. Category of native language
    Which clusters are most effective when the LM/LEP students' native language is historically related to English? When it is not?

2. Effects of specific service characteristics

    a. Using students' native language in teaching academic subjects

        1) What are the effects of using the student's native language in teaching academic subjects?

        2) How are the effects of the student's level of oral proficiency in the native language related to teaching academic subjects in the student's native language?

    b. Teaching reading of native language before teaching reading of English

        1) At the end of grade 6, how will students for whom the introduction of English reading was delayed while they were taught to read in their native language compare with students for whom reading in English was not postponed?

        2) To what extent does the effect of postponing instruction in reading English while the child learns to read in his native language first depend on

            a) The degree of lexical and orthographic similarity between the native language and English?

            b) Initial oral proficiency in the native language?

            c) General academic aptitude?

    c. Using "controlled" English vocabulary in instruction
    To what extent does the use of "special English" for instruction affect LM/LEP student achievement in:

        1) The content area?

        2) English?

    d. Styles of using two languages in instruction
    In the transition from the use of native language in instruction to 100 % English, which is more effective, a slow shift or a rapid shift?

    e. Subjects taught
    What are the effects of teaching the child's native language as a subject of instruction rather than merely using it as the medium of instruction?

3. Effect of school, classroom or teacher characteristics

    a. Linguistic composition of the student population

        1) Which clusters are the most effective when the child is in a school where there are few or no other children in his/her age group who speak the same language?

        2) Which clusters are most effective when the child is in a classroom where there are many other children in his/her age group who speak the same language?

    b. Untrained teachers
    What are the effects of untrained teachers by service clusters?

C. What are the effects of having English proficient students in LM/LEP classrooms on the achievement and English language acquisition of LM/LEP students?

1. What are the effects when the English proficient students come from a language minority background?
2. What are the effects when the English proficient students come from a native English speaking background?

REFERENCES

There are several good introductory books on samples surveys. Cochran (1977), Yates (1981), and Kish (1965) all provide thorough introductions to the entire field of the design and analysis of sample surveys. The book by Kasprzyk et al. (1987) discusses the issues of longitudinal surveys with particular attention to nonresponse adjustments and modeling considerations. Skinner, Holt, and Smith (1989) discuss methods for looking at complex surveys and pay special attention to issues of bias (in the statistical sense) and modeling structured populations. Groves (1989) provides a detailed discussion of issues related to survey errors and survey costs and includes an extensive discussion of problems with coverage and coverage error of samples together with concerns related to nonresponse. Little and Rubin (1987) is a basic reference for statistical analyses with missing data, both in experiments and sample surveys. Finally, Duncan (1975) is an early and invaluable reference for the latent and structural equation models used in path analysis.

Burkheimer, Jr., G. J., Conger, A. J., Dunteman, G. H., Elliott, B. G., and Mowbray, K. A. (1989) Effectiveness of services for language-minority limited-english-proficient students (2 vols). Technical report, Research Triangle Institute, Research Triangle Park, N.C.

Chambers, J. M., Cleveland, W. S., Kleiner, B., and Tukey, P. A. (1983) *Graphical Methods for Data Analysis*. Belmont, Calif.:   Wadsworth International Group.

Cochran, W. G. (1977) *Sampling Techniques* (third ed.). New York: John Wiley.

Development Associates (1984a) The descriptive phase report of the national longitudinal study of the effectiveness of services for LMLEP students. Technical report, Development Associates Inc., Arlington, Va.

Development Associates (1984b) Overview of the research design plans for the national longitudinal study study of the effectiveness of services for LMLEP students, with appendices. Technical report, Development Associates Inc., Arlington, Va.

Development Associates (1986) Year 1 report of the longitudinal phase. Technical report, Development Associates Inc., Arlington, Va.

Duncan, O. D. (1975) *Introduction to Structural Equation Models*. New York: Academic Press.

Groves, R. M. (1989) *Survey Errors and Survey Costs*. New York: John Wiley.

Kasprzyk, D., Duncan, G., Kalton, G., and Singh, M. P. (1987) *Panel Surveys*. New York: John Wiley.

Kish, L. (1965) *Survey Sampling*. New York: John Wiley.

Little, R. J. A., and Rubin, D. B. (1987) *Statistical Analysis with Missing Data*. New York: John Wiley.

Madow, W. G., Nisselson, J., and Olkin, I., eds. (1983) *Incomplete Data in Sample Surveys, Volume 1: Report and Case Studies*. Panel on Incomplete Data, Committee on National Statistics, Commission on Behavioral and Social Sciences and Education, National Research Council. New York: Academic Press.

Miller, R. G. (1981) *Simultaneous Statistical Inference* (second ed.). New York: Springer Verlag.

Skinner, C. J., Holt, D., and Smith, T. M. F. (1989) *Analysis of Complex Surveys*. New York: John Wiley.

Spencer, B. D., and Foran, W. (1991) Sampling probabilities for aggregations, with applications to NELS:88 and other educational longitudinal surveys. *Journal of Educational Statistics*, 16(1), 21–34.

U.S. Department of Education (1991) *The Condition of Bilingual Education in the Nation: A Report to the Congress and the President*. Office of the Secretary. Washington, D.C.: U.S. Department of Education.

Yates, F. (1981) *Sampling Methods for Censuses and Surveys* (fourth ed.). New York: Macmillan.

4

The Immersion Study

OVERVIEW

Comparing the Effects of Three Approaches to Bilingual Education

A treatment is an intervention or program that may be applied to or withheld from any individual in a population. In the simplest of settings, a treatment is a discrete event, performed briefly in the same way for all individuals; for instance, the injection of the Salk polio vaccine is a treatment in this sense. Quite often, however, a treatment is more complex, extending over a period of years, with many individuals involved in its delivery. This is particularly common in the field of education, though it is also common in caring for the chronically ill and in preventive medicine. Studies of such complex treatments inevitably and unavoidably encounter various difficulties concerning the definition, nature, and stability of the treatments. This section discusses these issues as they arose in the Immersion Study and considers how they were addressed.

The Immersion Study was conceived as a comparison of three treatments, called Immersion, Early-exit, and Late-exit. The final report of the Immersion Study was published in two volumes (Ramirez et al., 1991a, 1991b; hereafter called the Immersion Report) states (1991a, page 32): "The primary objective of this study is to assess the relative effectiveness of structured English immersion strategy, early-exit, and late-exit transitional bilingual education programs." All three programs were intended for students who speak Spanish, but have limited ability to speak English. All three programs had, as one of their goals, teaching students English. The conceptual distinction between the treatments is described in the Immersion Report (1991a, Table 4), to which the reader should refer for a more detailed discussion. In abbreviated form, the distinction is essentially as follows:

- Immersion: All instruction is in English, though the teacher is bilingual and may use Spanish in informal conversations and when clarifying directions. Students leave the program as soon as they have demonstrated proficiency in English, typically after 2–3 years.
- Early-exit: The teacher uses both Spanish and English in instruction, though content areas are taught in English. There may be instruction in Spanish-language skills, but the emphasis is on developing English-language skills. Students leave the program as soon as they have demonstrated proficiency in English, typically after 2–3 years.
- Late-exit: Students are taught both Spanish and English language skills, and both languages are used for instruction. All students leave the program at the end of the fifth or sixth grade.

As a basis for comparing and contrasting the panel's analysis of the Immersion Study, we present first the summary prepared by the U.S. Department of Education (U.S. Department of Education, 1991).

The Longitudinal Study of Structured English Immersion Strategy, Early-Exit and Late-Exit Transitional Bilingual Education Programs

This study compared the relative effectiveness of two alternative programs (structured English immersion and late-exit transitional bilingual education) with that of early-exit transitional bilingual education programs. The intent of the report is to describe characteristics of the instructional treatments and to identify similarities and differences among the three instructional approaches. Identifying such differences and similarities will help determine how changes in student achievement can be attributed to various instructional techniques.

According to the study's final report (Ramirez et al., 1991a, 1991b):

- The three programs represent three distinct instructional models. The participating teachers demonstrated and sustained language-use patterns that were faithful to the respective models, and the differences in student performance were overall attributable to differences in those approaches rather than to student, or other critical characteristics.
- Notwithstanding the programmatic differences, there were important and surprising similarities. Classroom activities tended to be teacher-directed, with limited student opportunities to produce language. Students produced language only when directly working with a teacher and then only in response to teacher initiations. Across all programs, teacher questions were typically low-level requests for simple information recall. The strategies used made for a passive learning environment which placed limits on students' opportunities to produce language and develop more complex language and conceptual skills.
- On the average, teachers in all three programs had sufficiently high oral English language skills to teach effectively in English, but only the Late-exit program had teachers with Spanish oral language skills that were sufficiently high to effectively teach in Spanish.
- Regarding relative impact, after four years in their respective programs,

limited English-proficient students in immersion strategy and early-exit programs demonstrated comparable skills in mathematics, language and reading when tested in English. There were differences among the three late-exit sites in achievement level in the same subjects: students in the site with the most use of Spanish and the site with the most use of English ended Grade six with the same skills in English language and reading; students in the two late-exit sites that used the most Spanish posted higher growth in mathematics skills than the site which abruptly transitioned into almost all English instruction. Students in all three programs realized a growth in English language and reading skills that was as fast or faster than the norming population.

• Parental involvement, particularly in length of time spent helping students with homework, appears to be greatest in the Late-exit programs. This suggests that schools should explore how they might use the home language of their students to engage parents in the schooling of their children.

Treatments and Treatment Effects

The effect of a treatment on one student is defined in terms of the responses that the student would exhibit under alternative treatments. Each student has a potential response that would be observed under each treatment. For instance, if the outcome is a score on a test of reading in English, each student has three potential scores: a score, y_I, that this student would produce if the student were placed in an immersion program; a score, y_E, that this student would produce if placed in an early-exit program; and a score, y_L, that this student would produce if placed in a late-exit program. If $y_L > y_E$, then this particular student would achieve a higher reading score if placed in a late-exit program than if placed in an early-exit program, and the difference, $y_L - y_E$, is the effect on this one student of applying the late-exit program rather than the early-exit program.

If z stands for the program a student actually receives, then $z = I$ if the student is placed in an immersion program, $z = E$ for an early-exit program, and $z = L$ for a late-exit program. Each student has a value of z. Each student is of course placed in only one program. Thus, for each student, y_I is observed only if the student is placed in an immersion program, that is, only if $z = I$; y_E is observed only in an early-exit program, that is, only if $z = E$; and y_L is observed only in a late-exit program, that is, only if $z = L$. As a result, the effect of a program on an individual student, say $y_L - y_E$, may never be calculated. Rather, treatment effects must be estimated for groups of students by comparing those who received different treatments (see "Data Analysis and Interpretation," below).

The Immersion Study did not create programs with prescribed characteristics, but rather searched the country to find programs that fit one of the three categories, Immersion, Early-exit, or Late-exit. The search and classification are described in Chapter 2 of Volume I of the Immersion Report. Immersion and Late-exit Programs are comparatively rare and were the basis for the search.

Table 4–1 shows the structure of the Immersion Study. Note that Late-exit

TABLE 4-1   Structure of the Immersion Study

Site	State	Immersion	Early-exit	Late-exit
A	TX	X	X	
B	CA	X	X	
C	CA	X	X	
D	FL			X
E	NY			X
F	TX	X	X	
G	NY			X
H	NJ	X		
I	TX		X	

SOURCE: Ramirez et al. (1991a, Table 5, page 39)

Programs do not appear in the same school district as other programs, while Immersion and Early-exit Programs do appear in the same district, and sometimes in the same school. The report states (Ramirez et al., 1991a, page 39): "The late-exit transitional bilingual program represented a district-wide policy"

A treatment, program, or intervention typically has many aspects—some of which are explicitly intended while others occur unintentionally. A student who receives the treatment is exposed to all of its aspects. At times, one may be able to say with confidence that a treatment has had a particular effect and yet be unable to say which aspect of the treatment produced the effect.

Since the programs in the Immersion Study were found and not created to specifications, the programs have aspects that were not part of the definitions of the treatments given earlier. For instance, the Immersion Report notes that more teachers in Late-exit Programs were Hispanic or knew more Spanish than in other programs. Also, teachers in the Late-exit Programs were "better educated and have more specialized training to work with language minority children than teachers in immersion strategy or early-exit programs" (Ramirez et al., 1991a, page 186). Specifically, substantially more teachers in the Late-exit Programs had master's degrees. These features of the Late-exit Program are not part of its intended definition, but they are aspects of the program and thus of the treatments actually received by the students.

The Immersion Report does quite a good job of documenting unintended aspects of the programs. Even with this good effort, however, it is possible and perhaps likely, that the programs differ in still other unintended ways that were not observed. These, too, are inextricable parts of the treatments.

To the extent that the Immersion Study is a horse race between existing programs as they are currently implemented, the issue of unintended features of the programs is not a major problem. It becomes a significant problem if one wants to go beyond declaring a winner or declaring a tie to attributing the victory or tie to the intended features of the program and not to the unintended features. A horse race may have a clear winner while providing limited information about what made that horse win. The panels notes, however, that the horse race aspect of the Immersion Study is neither uninteresting nor irrelevant for policy. A clear winner might tell policy makers that they want more programs "like that," while leaving us in doubt about the essential features of a program "like that" but eager to try to duplicate all of the features.

In a study with many more sites than the Immersion Study, or with fewer unintended aspects of programs, it might be possible to use analytical procedures to formulate an educated guess about which aspects of programs contributed to their performance; at least, this might be possible for the aspects that were measured and recorded. In the Immersion Study, however, it is not clear, and perhaps not likely, that such analyses would yield much.

In addition to unintended aspects of the three different programs, there are also unintended differences in implementation of the "same" program at different sites. Again, the Immersion Report does an admirable job of describing some of these differences. For instance, the report states (Ramirez et al., 1991a): "...only teachers in the immersion strategy program sites are homogeneous in their [near exclusive] use of English." Other strategies varied considerably in their use of English: for example, "Early-exit site F classrooms are practically indistinguishable from immersion strategy classrooms in that teachers at this site also use English almost exclusively ..." Other variations are also described.

Although the Immersion Study was just described as a horse race between existing programs having both intended and unintended aspects, it is more accurate to describe parts of the Immersion Study as several separate horse races between related but not identical treatments.

Who Was Measured? What Was Measured? When Was It Measured?

In an ideal educational experiment or observational study, well-defined groups of students receive each treatment, and outcomes are available for all students in each group. This ideal is often difficult to achieve when students are studied for a long time.

The Immersion Report discusses losses of students over time (Ramirez et al., 1991a, pages 369–376). Table 4–2 is adapted from that discussion. Some students left the study without being reclassified as fully English proficient (FEP), that is, they left the study in the "middle." Almost all of the students who left early transferred to a class, school, or district that was not part of the Immersion Study or left for unknown reasons. In all three groups, more than one-half of the students left the study early. Ramirez et al. (1991b, page 20) says:

> Attrition of the student from the study meant no additional test scores could be obtained for that student. The predominant reason for attrition was that the student's family moved outside the district. Students who were mainstreamed were not considered to have left the study: test scores for mainstreamed study students are not missing by design.

TABLE 4–2   Students Leaving the Studies

| | Program | | |
Students	Immersion	Early-exit	Late-exit
Total Number in Each Program	749	939	664
Number Exiting the Study Without Being Reclassified as FEP	423	486	414
Percent	56%	52%	62%

Despite this statement, more than 30 percent of the students who left early changed classes or schools without leaving the school district (Ramirez et al., 1991a, Table 168).

Losses of this kind are not uncommon in educational investigations. The losses here are less severe than those in the Longitudinal Study (see Chapter 3). Nonetheless, from the two volumes of the report, it is difficult to appraise the impact of the loss of so many students. If the students who left were similar to those who remained, then the impact might be small. If similar students left each program, but they differed from those who remained, this might alter the general level of results without favoring any program to the detriment of others. For instance, this situation might happen if students left programs *only* because their parents moved. It is also possible, however, that the students leaving one program differ from those leaving another; this might happen if some students or parents had strong feelings about the programs. An additional analysis of considerable interest might have been to compare the background or baseline characteristics of students in six groups categorized by leaving or staying in each of the three programs and attempting to adjust the results for any observed differences.

The application of a treatment occurs at a specific time. Measurements made prior to the start of treatment might not be affected by the treatment; in this report such quantities are labeled as covariates (this is a more restrictive use of the term than might be occur in other settings). Quantities measured after the start of treatment may be affected by the treatment; such quantities are labeled as outcomes. The formal distinction can be related to the discussion above: for each student, a covariate takes a single value, but an outcome has three potential values for each student, depending on the treatment received by the student.

When the distinction between outcomes and covariates is ignored, analytical procedures may introduce biases into comparisons where none existed previously. Specifically, if an outcome is treated as a covariate—that is, if adjustments are made for an outcome variable—it may distort the actual effects of a treatment, even in randomized experiments.

In the Immersion Study, adjustments for outcomes appear in three guises.

First, pretest scores for kindergarten students are not actually pretest scores; they were not obtained prior to the start of treatment, but, rather, in the early part of kindergarten. This first adjustment attempt would be fairly unimportant if programs were to take years to have material effects, a possibility that is reasonable but not certain. In the absence of genuine pretest scores, the researchers' decision to use early kindergarten scores instead of pretest scores was probably the best alternative.

In the second guise, the "number of days absent" is actually an outcome, perhaps an important one, that may have been affected by the treatments if students found one program particularly frustrating or satisfying. The Immersion Study uses this variable as a covariate (Ramirez et al., 1991b, page 81). If one of the program treatments had a dramatic effect on this variable, adjusting for it—that is, treating it as a covariate—might distort the treatment effect. The researchers should have conducted simple analyses to investigate the possible effects of the programs on the "number of days absent" and should have considered the possible impact of such effects on their adjustments. Simple methods exist to do this; one reference is Rosenbaum (1984, section 4.3).

The third guise in which adjustment for outcomes occurs is discussed in connection with the cohort structure of the study. The study had a fairly complex cohort structure (Ramirez et al., 1991a, page 41), with six different cohorts of students in the first year of data collection; see Table 4–3.

Specifically, a group or cohort of children was followed, beginning in kindergarten, for each of the three programs or treatments. For Immersion and Early-exit Programs, an additional cohort was followed, beginning in first grade. For Late-exit Programs, a cohort was followed, beginning in third grade.

As the authors noted (Ramirez et al., 1991a, page 32), "the primary objective of this study is to assess the relative effectiveness of structured English immersion strategy, early-exit, and late-exit transitional bilingual education programs." The third-grade Late-exit cohort is of no use for this main objective, though it may have other appropriate uses.

The panel's impression from the Immersion Report is that students in both of the first-grade cohorts had also often been in Immersion or Early-exit Programs in kindergarten, and it is only the observation of these children that begins in first

TABLE 4–3 First Year Study Cohorts by Grade

	Program		
Kindergarten	Kindergarten	1st	3rd
Immersion	X	X	
Early-exit	X	X	
Late-exit	X		X

grade. The real problem is that we do not know which program they were in, which limits the usefulness of the first grade cohorts for the "primary objective." First graders had been exposed to a treatment, and may have been affected by it, for more than a year before any measurements were recorded. As a result, all measurements on these students might, in principle, have been affected by the treatment. There are no covariates or baseline measurements. As a result, it is not possible to examine the comparability of the first-grade cohorts prior to treatment or to use covariates to adjust for baseline differences. It is like watching a baseball game beginning in the fifth inning: if you are not told the score from prior innings, nothing you see can tell you who is winning the game.

This concern about comparability occurs frequently in observational studies, in contrast to randomized experiments, because the treatment groups often differ systematically and substantially prior to treatment. The panel therefore concludes that the first-grade cohorts are of limited use for the "primary objective" of the Immersion Study.

DATA ANALYSIS AND INTERPRETATION

Comparability of Treatment Groups: Overt and Hidden Biases

In randomized experiments, the random assignment of students to treatment groups is intended to ensure that the students in different groups are comparable prior to the start of treatment. Somewhat more precisely, conventional statistical procedures applied to the results from experiments take into account the kinds of noncomparability that random assignment may create. In contrast, in observational studies the students in different treatment groups may not have been comparable prior to the start of treatment. Indeed, there is ample evidence of this in the Immersion Study. A major focus of the analytical effort in an observational study is distinguishing the actual effects of the treatments from the initial lack of comparability of the treatment groups. This section discusses the comparability of the groups in the Immersion Study, the adjustments made for noncomparability or bias, and the detection and assessment of hidden biases that were not adjusted for.

By long and established statistical tradition, noncomparability of treatment groups is referred to as "bias," a somewhat unfortunate term. In nontechnical English, the word "bias" suggests deliberate malfeasance, but this meaning is not intended in the present context. Biases afflict most observational studies, and good researchers recognize their probably existence and attempt to adjust for them. The Immersion Study included such attempted adjustments.

An *overt bias* is one that is visible in the data at hand. A *hidden bias* is one that is not observed, measured, or recorded. Care is needed to avoid mistaking either overt or hidden biases for effects of the treatments. This section first presents examples of overt biases in the Immersion Study; it then discusses the adjustments for them and notes the lack of attention to sensitivity to hidden biases.

TABLE 4–4   Gross Family Income of Study Students

	Program		
Family Income	Immersion	Early-exit	Late-exit
< $7,500	25.4%	19.7%	40.7%
≥ $20,000	19.1%	21.3%	8.9%

SOURCE: Ramirez et al. (1991a, Table 148, page 351)

The Immersion Study contains many overt biases. Four examples serve to illustrate the point. Tables 4–4 to 4–6 provide information about characteristics of the families in the different programs. The tables have an implicit row of "other" so that the columns add up to 100 percent. The first example concerns family income. Table 4–4 compares the three treatment groups in terms of gross family income. Although family income is not high in any group, children in Late-exit Programs tend to come from families with substantially lower incomes than children in other programs.

The second and third examples concern the proportion of parents receiving Aid to Families with Dependent Children (AFDC) and the proportion of children attending preschool; see Table 4–5. Once again, the most dramatic differences are those between the Late-exit Programs and the other programs. Far more parents of students in Late-exit Programs receive AFDC; far fewer children in Late-exit Programs attended preschool.

The fourth example of an overt bias compares the treatment groups in terms of newspapers that the students' parents regularly receive. Here, the big difference is in the receipt of Spanish-language newspapers, which is far more common among the parents of students in Late-exit Programs; see Table 4–6.

In many instances, the Immersion and Early-exit groups appear more comparable to each other than either group is to the Late-exit group. It is likely that this is not an accident: Immersion and Early-exit Programs were typically selected from the same school district, and often from the same school, while Late-exit Programs typically came from other districts (see Table 4–1 above). This issue

TABLE 4–5   AFDC Receipt and Preschool Attendance

	Program		
Characteristic	Immersion	Early-exit	Late-exit
AFDC	16.8%	12.7%	47.2%
Attended Preschool	44.4%	37.0%	29.4%

SOURCE: Ramirez et al. (1991a, Tables 149 and 150, pages 352 and 354)

TABLE 4–6   Parents Newspaper Receipt, by Language

	Program		
Newspaper Language	Immersion	Early-exit	Late-exit
English	42.8%	48.0%	42.9%
Spanish	28.0%	27.7%	54.1%

SOURCE: Ramirez et al. (1991a, Table 152, page 356)

turns out to be important for the interpretation of the Immersion Study, because there appear to be substantial differences between schools and school districts, or perhaps differences between the communities served by different schools. This point is elaborated on in the next section. In short, there are many overt biases: the groups differ prior to treatment in many ways we can see, and these differences were not controlled for.

Adjusting for Overt Biases

As discussed above, the three treatment or program groups differed prior to the commencement of the treatment in various ways identifiable in the available data. The Immersion Report includes an attempt to handle these differences by using covariance adjustment, a standard statistical approach. These analyses divide into three groups, described in Chapters 3–5 of Volume II of the Immersion Report. The first group (in Chapter 3) makes comparisons of two different programs in the same school. The second group (in Chapter 4) makes comparisons of two programs in the same school district, but not necessarily in the same school. The third group (Chapter 5) makes comparisons that involve programs in different school districts. Unfortunately, as we have noted, Late-exit Programs always appear alone, in a district without other study programs. As a result, comparisons involving Late-exit Programs are always in the third group.

As the Immersion Report notes (Ramirez et al., 1991b, page 93):

> When a single school has both programs, the [Immersion] and [Early-exit] programs can be compared without concern that differences between schools or districts are affecting results. In addition, controlling for school effectively controls for the attributes of the community served by the school.

Elsewhere, the report states (page 44):

> The analyses that may be performed to evaluate the nominal program are severely limited by the study design, which in turn was severely limited by the paucity of [Immersion] and [Late-exit] programs. Despite an extensive national search, only a handful of immersion strategy and late-exit programs were identified. Essentially all of the districts with [Immersion] and [Late-exit] programs agreed to participate in the study. However, no district with a late-exit program had any other program. This fact, together with the limited

number of districts with late-exit programs, makes comparison of the [Late-exit] program with the [Immersion] and [Early-exit] programs extremely difficult. That is, one cannot control for district or school level differences.

The panel agrees with these observations and concurs with the authors of the report that the first group of analyses is the most credible for the reasons given. This is a key point in interpreting the results of the Immersion Study. In addition, the panel generally regards the analyses of kindergarten through first grade as more compelling than analyses of first through third grades.

The Most Compelling Comparisons: Programs in the Same School for Grades K–1

For the K–1 analyses in the same school that the panel finds most compelling, there were four major conclusions in the Immersion Report:

- Although the immersion strategy students tend to score five or six points lower than early-exit students on the *mathematics* subtest, the difference is not statistically significant (page 103).
- Although the immersion strategy students tend to score four to five points higher than early-exit students on the *language* subtest, the difference is not statistically significant (page 105).
- The immersion strategy students tend to score eight to nine points lower than early-exit students on the *reading* subtest, and the difference is statistically significant at the .05 level (page 108).
- The subsequent analyses using the reduced group of students with pretest scores produce qualitatively similar results, whether or not adjustments are made for pretest scores, though the reading difference is somewhat larger for this group (pages 108–127).

Each of these conclusions is based on several analyses that are usually reasonably consistent. Thus, when comparing Immersion and Early-exit Programs in the most compelling portion of the data, there is little indication of differences in mathematics or language scores, but there is some evidence of a difference in reading that favors Early-exit Programs.

What remains is to appraise the evidence that this difference is an effect actually produced by the Early-exit Program. There are three issues: (1) Are there substantial problems in the analytical technique used? (2) Is there evidence specifically presented in the Immersion Report that would lead one to doubt that the difference is an actual effect? (3) Are there sources of uncertainty that are not addressed in the report? All of the panels' answers come from its reading of the Immersion Report, rather than from independent analyses or a direct review of the data.

Concerning the first issue, the panel found no indication of substantial problems in the covariance adjustments that form the basis for the above observations. One might reasonably object to features of some of the reported regression analyses, but the results are highly consistent across a number of different analyses, and thus concerns about a few regression analyses would be unlikely to materially affect the conclusions. The Immersion Report gives no indication that the regression models were checked using residual analysis and related techniques, but it is unlikely that they would alter the conclusions. The report might have done a better job of documenting the selection of covariates for the analyses, but again, the results are quite consistent across a number of analyses with different choices of covariates.

Concerning the second issue, the panel found no evidence that would lead it to doubt that the difference in reading scores is an actual effect. In other words, there appear to be no internal inconsistencies or unexplained disparities in the data as presented in the report that would lead one to doubt that the difference is a real effect.

Concerning the third issue, there are sources of uncertainty or potential problems that are not addressed. For example, most students left the program early. Also, students who appear similar in observed ways may nonetheless differ in unobserved ways, that is, there may be hidden biases. To some extent, there are unavoidable sources of uncertainty in nonexperimental studies of this sort, and the report falls short of addressing all of these sources of uncertainty. Very little is done to explore or address issues surrounding the extensive incomplete data: Are the students who left the program early similar to those who stayed? Although a complete and certain answer is not possible, simple analyses of the data may contain a partial answer. Finally, the Immersion Report makes no effort to consider the possible impact of unobserved differences between students. Could small unobserved differences between students—that is, small hidden biases—account for the difference in reading scores? Or would it take large hidden biases? How sensitive are the conclusions to hidden bias? Again, there are simple analyses might provide an answer here.

In summary, nothing presented in the Immersion Report leads the panel to doubt the report's conclusion that the Early-exit Programs produce greater achievement than Immersion Programs in reading for K–1 students; however, uncertainties attenuate this conclusion, and these uncertainties might have been partially reduced or at least clarified with fairly simple additional analyses. Nonetheless, the panel concluded this analysis is the most compelling portion of the Immersion Report and judges the report's conclusion to be reasonably credible.

Growth Curve Analyses for Grades 1–3: Watching the Second Half of the Ball Game

The Immersion Report presents a number of growth curve analyses for information on grades 1–3. These analyses look at students' test scores in first grade and see how they change from then until third grade. The panel did not find these analyses to be intuitively compelling in light of potential previous differences among students. Specifically, the level of performance in first grade reflects two very different things: the differences between students prior to the start of the programs, that is, prior to kindergarten, and differences between students' development during kindergarten and first grade, including effects of the bilin-

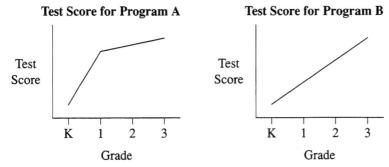

FIGURE 4–1 Hypothetical Student Growth Curves

gual programs under study. A student with better than average performance in first grade may either have started school with various advantages or have developed faster, perhaps due to a good program. These two possible cases are not distinguished in the growth curve analyses.

Figure 4–1 illustrates this point with two hypothetical growth curves for two students in two hypothetical programs (A and B). Both children start in exactly the same place in kindergarten. Both children end up in exactly the same place at the end of third grade. The two programs are equally effective in terms of third-grade achievement. However, if one focuses on grades 1–3, program B looks much more effective. After all, the student in program B was a long way behind in first grade, but has caught up by third grade. This outcome appears to be great progress attributable to program B. If one focuses also on K–1 one sees that the student in program B did less well at first and then merely made up for lost ground in grades 1–3. There are innumerable hypothetical pictures like this one that demonstrate that one *cannnot* measure total accomplishment by looking only at accomplishment in the second half of a process.

If one is interested in performance in third grade, one might look at performance in third grade, with an adjustment for baseline differences in kindergarten. If one is compelled to look at growth curves, the growth curves must extend from kindergarten to third grade; they cannot start at grade one. One needs to be careful that data limitations, such as those imposed by the cohort structure, do not lead to inappropriate analyses.

Programs in Different Schools: Comparing Students Who Are Not Comparable

The comparison of Immersion and Early-exit Programs involved schools that contain only one of the programs. The report states (Ramirez et al., 1991b, pages 171–172):

> Even after including the background variables in the model, statistically significant school effects were found ... The presence of differences among the one-program schools greatly complicates the comparison of the immersion strategy and early-exit programs. The one-program school analyses cannot

control for school effects because school is confounded with program. As a result, we cannot directly separate out school effects from program effects.

Again, the panel agrees with this conclusion.

The Immersion Report goes on to say that differences in test performance among schools in the same district and program are large and that differences between districts are not much greater than expected based on differences between schools in the same district; the associated analyses are not presented. The analyses in Chapter 4 of Volume II of the report, however, show point estimates of differences between districts that are much larger than point estimates of program effects (often the coefficients of indicator variables representing districts or schools are an order of magnitude larger than the coefficient of the indicator variable for programs). Because differences in test scores between schools with the same program are large, the much smaller difference between the group of schools with Immersion Programs and the group of schools with Early-exit Programs does not necessarily reflect a difference in the programs: it might very easily be part of the substantial difference between schools and the communities they serve.

This issue about the magnitude of effects can be formalized as follows: multiple schools with the same program may be thought of as multiple control groups, and the comparison of these schools may be thought of as a test for hidden bias. From this perspective, there is ample evidence of hidden bias. The Immersion Report takes a different view, building a *random-effects* model for school-to-school differences and comparing the program difference to the variability between schools. One might argue about which perspective is more appropriate; however, in this case, both approaches tend to give the same answer. Given the large differences between schools with the same type of program, it is not possible to say much about the effectiveness of programs in different schools. Despite the very large number of statistical tests for program differences that were performed, very few yielded significant differences (Ramirez et al., 1991b, page 286): "Almost no program differences were found among the one-program schools." Furthermore, the Immersion Report summarizes (page 282):

> Perhaps the most important result of the analyses of one-program schools is that school-to-school differences are large even within the same district and program. Any program differences are small compared to school differences.

Given that the school-to-school differences are important to the interpretation of the study result, it would have been helpful if the report had presented more information about these differences. Nonetheless, the panel concluded that it is unlikely that this added information would alter the basic finding.

Late-Exit Programs Are Not Compared with Other Programs Using Conventional Analytical Methods

The analysis of the Late-exit Program (in Chapter 5 of Volume II) uses the same conventional methods as Chapters 3 and 4; however, it does not compare Late-exit Programs to Immersion and Early-exit Programs. The report states (Ramirez et al., 1991b, page 287):

The late-exit students were analyzed separately in large part because the districts with late-exit programs had implemented no alternative programs. This makes it impossible to compare students in the late-exit program with students in other programs while controlling for district differences.

Thus, the data on the Late-exit Programs do not contribute to the primary objective of the study, at least from the perspective of conventional methods of statistical analysis. The Immersion Report is probably correct that it is not possible to provide a reasonable comparison of a Late-exit Program in one district with an Immersion or Early-exit Program in another district.

In an attempt to mitigate this seemingly overwhelming problem, the researchers abandoned conventional statistical analysis methods and switched to TAMP (trajectory analysis of matched percentiles) analyses and compared students in different districts (Chapter 6 of Volume II). The panel does not share their view that the differences between districts can be addressed by switching to a different analytical technique even though it appreciates the ingenuity of the TAMP approach (see Appendix B). The TAMP analysis does provide an exploratory method for comparing the changes in multiple populations, but one can only draw inferences from the TAMP graphs if the populations are comparable. The TAMP methodology seems to have been used precisely because the populations were not directly comparable; hence, the conclusions drawn from the TAMP curves are dubious. Any inferences hinted at by a TAMP analysis would still need to be confirmed in a follow-up confirmatory study or analysis.

Sensitivity to Hidden Biases

The Immersion Report does little to investigate whether hidden biases might account for ostensible program effects. For instance, one might ask how much hidden bias would need to be present to account for the difference in reading scores in Immersion and Early-exit Programs? Fairly simple calculations suffice to answer this. Since it is difficult, if not impossible, to assure that small hidden biases are absent, the reader should be warned whether small biases would alter the conclusion. On the other hand, if only very large biases are required to alter the conclusions, the reader would then place greater confidence in the conclusions. A nontechnical discussion of these issues is given in Rosenbaum (1991), and specific methods are illustrated in Rosenbaum (1986, page 219), Rosenbaum and Kreiger (1990), and Rosenbaum and Rubin (1983).

Unit of Analysis: How Far Can One Generalize?

The student is the "unit of analysis" in analyses throughout the Immersion Study, and to this point the panel has adopted the same view. This choice of the unit of analysis has significant consequences for the interpretation of results. Alternative units of analysis would be the classroom, the school, or the school district. The phrase "unit of analysis" is not particularly suggestive of the nature of the issues involved, which are both technical and subject to some debate among statisticians. This section briefly outlines these issues and then discusses their implications for the interpretation of the Immersion Study.

One common view of the "unit of analysis" issue takes the student as the unit of analysis in order to make statements that generalize to other students, that is, to students not in the Immersion Study. If the student is the unit of analysis, however, then implicitly there is no desire to generalize to other classrooms or teachers, to other schools, or to other school districts. In other words, with the student as the unit of analysis, one asks: "What can one say about what would happen if more students in the same schools attended the same classes with the same teachers?" With the student as the unit of analysis one does *not* usually ask: "What can one say about what would happen if more students in the other schools attended similar classes with different teachers?" For this question one would take the school as the unit of analysis. In this view, there is no right or wrong choice of a unit of analysis, but each choice is tied both to certain analyses and to certain questions. If one wanted to generalize to other teachers, not those specifically in the Immersion Study, then one would have needed a different unit of analysis and different analytical methods and one would be answering a different question. An unstated premise underpinning this view is that variation or uncertainty arises in statistics principally through sampling: that is, statistical methods are needed for inference because one observes only part of the population, for example, some but not all of the students or some but not all of the teachers.

An alternative perspective sees observational studies such as the Immersion Study as more closely tied to experiments than to sample surveys. In the traditional literature on randomization in experiments, statistical methods are needed for inference not because one observes only part of the population, but because one observes each individual under only one treatment, that is, one observes only one of y_I, y_E, or y_L. In this traditional statistical literature, which dates back to the creator of randomized experiments, Sir R. A. Fisher, one does not assume that the individuals included in an experiment are a sample from a population, and one confines inferences to effects of the treatments on individuals in the study; randomization permits inferences about the effects caused by the treatments, even though individual treatment effects, such as $y_I - y_E$, can never be calculated. In somewhat common statistical parlance, the randomization confers *internal validity* to generalizations of inferences from an experiment. For inferences from observational studies that are used in lieu of experiments, one should therefore be loath to adopt a broader form of generalization. To go from this internal validity to the *external validity* of inferences for units outside the study would require the random selection of the units within the study from the larger population of interest.

Since the units (students) within other units in the Immersion Study were not drawn at random, the panel believes that it is appropriate, at least at the outset, to restrict attention to an analysis that attends to the internal structure. Then the issue of the unit of analysis divides into three separate questions: "How were treatments assigned to students?" "Do students 'interfere' with each other in the sense that the giving one student a particular treatment affects not only that student but other students as well?" "Are there different versions of the treatment?" The following discussion addresses these questions in turn.

First, how were treatments assigned to students? Were students in the same school divided into groups which received different treatments? In this case, the student would apparently be the unit of analysis. Or were all students in a given school or district given the same treatment? In this case, the school or district would be the unit of analysis. Both types of assignment appear to have occurred in the Immersion Study. Thus, the unit of analysis is the student in those schools that contain both Immersion and Early-exit Programs; but in schools or districts that contain only one program, the unit of analysis is the school or district. Once again, the Immersion Study's reported analyses of programs in the same school seem more appropriate and plausible than analyses that compare programs in different schools or districts.

Second, do students interfere with one another? Does the treatment given to one student affect other students indirectly? It is not possible to answer these questions with a study like the Immersion Study. It is possible, in principle, that students do interfere with each other. This might happen, for example, to a student if Spanish is spoken at home, if the student is rarely asked to speak in class, and when asked says little. In this case, the principal opportunity to practice English may come from speaking with other students. If a student's best friend receives a particular program, this might, in principle, affect the quiet student as well. Typically, a unit of analysis is selected so that units of the selected type do not interfere with one another: that is, units are chosen to formulate the problem so that interference does not arise. For example, students in different schools are not likely to interfere with one another to any significant degree. These observations would argue for the school as the unit of analysis. The alternative is to continue with the student as the unit of analysis but to try to address possible interference in some way. Although doing so is certainly possible, there is little help to be found in the statistical literature.

Third, are there versions of the treatment? As noted above, there do appear to have been different versions of different programs. If the Immersion Study is viewed as several separate horse races between related but not identical treatments (as suggested above), then the student may be the appropriate unit of analysis. If, instead, there is a desire to use the variation between versions of each treatment in an effort to describe variation between programs that may arise in the future, then the school or district has to be the unit of analysis. This latter view leads back to the discussion of the first view of "units of analysis" that began this section.

From a practical point of view, if the unit of analysis for the Immersion Study is anything but the student, the statistician has little with which to work. For instance, if the site is the unit of analysis, the sample size in the Late-exit group is only three sites.

With the student as the unit of analysis, the panel has two major conclusions about what can be learned from the Immersion Study. First, comparisons of two or more programs within the same school can reasonably view the student as the unit of analysis, with a caveat. Such a comparison is a collection of separate contests between related but not identical treatments as they were implemented in certain specific schools; it provides unconfirmed suggestions about how things would be different with different teachers, in different school districts, or in programs with other incidental differences. Second, comparisons of programs in different schools could use the student as the unit of analysis only if variation in outcomes between schools and districts is adequately controlled by adjustments for covariates, but as discussed above ("Adjusting for Overt Biases"), this does not appear to have been done.

SUGGESTIONS FOR THE FUTURE

Further Analyses of the Current Data Set

The Department of Education provided the panel with data tapes for the Immersion Study; however, the panel was unable to successfully manipulate the data. There were several technical problems relating to the format of the data and the quality of the tape media that interfered with our efforts. We believe that the Immersion Study data are quite valuable and encourage the Department of Education to make the data publicly available in a form that is easy for researchers to use, while protecting confidentiality.

Several further analyses of the data from the Immersion Study would be especially useful in helping one to appraise the findings, particularly the one positive finding of evidence in support of superior reading performance in kindergarten and first-grade for students in Early-exit Programs in comparison to Immersion Programs. Three such analyses are of students who left the study early, of sensitivity to hidden bases, and of school-to-school variations.

Many students left the study early. It would be helpful to know more about how these students differed from those who stayed in the study. Since the panel believes the most credible data comes from the comparison of Immersion and Early-exit Programs in the same schools, information on students who left these schools and whether differences are related to Immersion versus Early-exit would be especially valuable. A simple analysis would describe the baseline characteristics of the students in the four groups:

	Program	
Characteristic	Immersion	Early-exit
Stayed in Program		
Left Program Early		

Another useful analysis would look at how sensitive the study conclusions are to hidden bias. Students who appear similar on the basis of observed characteristics may differ in ways not observed—there may be hidden bias. How much hidden bias would need to be present to account for the difference in reading scores in the Immersion and Early-exit Programs? Fairly simple calculations can be done to answer this question. Such sensitivity analyses would be a useful addition, particularly for the comparison of students in Immersion and Early-exit Programs in the same school.

A major issue in Chapters 4 and 5 of Volume II of the Immersion Report is the variation in results from school to school. This issue usually appears as part of complex analyses or is based on results not reported in detail. Some basic data summaries would give a clearer picture of what is happening among schools, even though such information is not likely to alter the basic conclusions of the report.

Suggestions for the Design of Future Studies

The panel's analysis of the Immersion Report leads us to propose several features for future studies. First, future studies should compare competing programs within the same schools. Given the variation in test performance between schools, or perhaps between the communities the schools serve, it is difficult to distinguish program effects from inherent differences between schools and communities when competing programs exist within different schools. Similarly, even within one school, it may be difficult to distinguish program effects from the effects of different teachers. In the Immersion Study, the most credible comparisons were of Immersion and Early-exit Programs in the same schools.

Second, more emphasis should be placed on comparability and data completeness in study designs. There is often a tradeoff between the quality and completeness of data and the degree to which the data represent the whole population of interest. It is easier to ensure data quality if one is working at only a few locations. It is easier to obtain relatively complete data if one selects a fairly stable community than if one studies a large number of typical but perhaps unstable communities. Data completeness is a major problem in both the Longitudinal Study and the Immersion Study. The panel believes the Department of Education, in the programs it supports on the evaluation of program effectiveness, places far too much emphasis on obtaining "representative" data, and not enough emphasis on obtaining complete, high-quality data for a more restrictive population of interest. The panel believes it is better to learn definitely what worked some place than to fail everywhere to learn what works.

National studies of the effects of programs would be much more valuable if more was known about the most effective local programs. One way to achieve this objective would be to work with several population laboratories, as described by Cochran (1965). This means identifying a few communities that are particularly suitable for study, even if they are not nationally representative. A good example of the use of a population laboratory is provided by the Framingham Heart Study. The community of Framingham, just west of Boston, Massachusetts, was selected for a major study of heart disease and related health conditions, not because it was a typical U.S. community, but because is was a stable community. The Framingham study provided a great deal of valuable data over a long period in part because it was not typical: few people moved away, and all the data came from one place, so there was high data quality and uniformity; only a relatively small number of local officials and physicians were involved in data collection; and so on.

A population laboratory for the evaluation of bilingual education programs would be a community that is unusually stable, with as little migration as possible. It is true that such a community may not be typical, but the panel notes that it is very difficult to study a migrant community over long periods of time. A good study community would also be eager to participate over an extended period, willing to expend effort to produce complete, high-quality data, and flexible about putting in place competing programs with different characteristics.

Third, ideally one would wish to *create* competing programs for study rather than to find existing programs. The panel believes strongly in turning the ideal into reality. Created programs would have fewer unintended features, so it would be clearer why they succeed or fail. Admittedly, creating programs is more expensive than finding them, but a great deal of money was spent on the Immersion Study, and only a restricted part of the data turned out to be of value. The amount of money spent, with limited benefit, on both the Immersion and Longitudinal Studies would have been sufficient to create a few carefully planned programs within two or three focused population laboratories. Thus, we are suggesting better deployment of allocated funds rather than increased funding.

Created programs have several advantages:

- Competing programs may be created in the same school, thereby avoiding one of the most serious problems in some of the current data from the Immersion and Longitudinal Studies.
- The characteristics of the programs can be created to maximize the clarity and impact of the study. For example, the Immersion and Late-exit Programs are polar opposite concepts—if there is a difference between programs, one would expect to see it between these two programs. The existing Immersion and Late-exit Programs are not in the same school district, however, so it hard to compare them. Rather, Immersion Programs were compared with Early-exit Programs, programs that are somewhat in the middle.
- Programs with the same name would actually be essentially the same program. In contrast, in the Immersion Study, programs called "immersion" differ from each other, as did programs called "early-exit" and "late-exit."
- Data collection could be built in as an essential part of the programs.

Creating programs requires cooperation by local schools, parents, and children. This cooperation might be somewhat easier to elicit if resources were available to make the competing experimental programs attractive. Reduced class size in the competing programs, teacher's aides, and adequate administrative support for the burdens of data collection are all ways to make competing programs attractive without favoring any particular program. Participants in such experimental programs should see their participation as yielding added resources, not just added responsibilities. Competing programs should be sufficiently attractive that many, if not most, parents and children would see participation in any of the competing programs as an improvement over previously available alternatives. In Chapter 5, the panel attempts to provide the groundwork for the discussions that must precede the creation of programs for future studies.

Fourth, the panel believes that, when possible, it is best to run true experiments, in which students are randomly assigned to competing programs within the same school. With experiments, randomization provides a statistical justification for drawing causal conclusions from estimates of differences in outcomes between students in different programs.

Random assignment has long been the norm in medical studies of new drugs, even for life-threatening conditions. This was not always the case and the shift to random assignment required great effort. A key feature for successful implementation of randomization in medical studies is that patients correctly perceive that the quality of care they will receive in either of the competing experimental treatments is at least as good as the care they would receive if they declined to participate. Experiments with human subjects are ethical and practical only when (1) the best treatment is not known, and (2) the competing treatments are all believed or hoped to be at least as beneficial as the standard treatments. In recent years ethical concerns about giving patients an inferior treatment have led to the institution of data, safety, and monitoring committees that stop trials early (and sometimes to an increased reluctance to launch trials) in the face of observational evidence that a new treatment is preferred. In bilingual education such an approach would mean that the competing programs should be seen by all involved as attractive in comparison with what is available outside the experiment and that the study should be designed with sufficient flexibility to allow for changing treatments if one of the programs is clearly superior.

Though randomization is highly desirable, it is not always practical or ethical. An attempt to randomize will fail when an experimenter cannot really control the assignment of treatments to subject. A well-conducted observational study can be of greater value than an unsuccessful attempt to conduct a randomized experiment.

REFERENCES

The definition of a treatment effect used in this chapter was suggested by Neyman (1923) and is now standard in the traditional statistical literature on experimental design; see, for example, Welch (1937), Wilk (1955), and Cox (1958a). Rubin (1974) discusses how the definition is used in the context of observational studies, and Cochran (1965) and Rubin (1984) discuss a broader array of issues of interpretation in such studies. Sir Ronald Fisher (1925) first showed that randomization in experiments provides a formal justification for basing causal inferences on the results of certain statistical procedures; see also Kempthorne (1952), Cox (1958b), and Rubin (1978). Rosenbaum (1984) discusses the consequences of treating outcomes as if they were covariates in the sense of treatments and treatment effects. Campbell (1969) and Rosenbaum (1987) describe the use of multiple control groups to detect hidden bias. Cornfield et al. (1959) provide an illustration of some of the kinds of sensitivity analyses suggested in this chapter. Other useful references on sensitivity include Rosenbaum (1986, 1991). Cox (1958b) discusses the issue of interference between units.

Campbell, D. (1969) Prospective: Artifact and control. In R. Rosenthal and R. Rosnow, eds., *Artifact in Behavioral Research*. New York: Academic Press.

Cochran, W. G. (1965) The planning of observational studies of human populations (with discussion). *Journal of the Royal Statistical Society, Series A*, 128, 124–135.

Cornfield, J., Haenszel, W., Hammond, E., and others (1959) Smoking and lung cancer: Recent evidence and a discussion of some questions. *Journal of the National Cancer Institute*, 22, 173–203.

Cox, D. R. (1958a) The interpretation of the effects of non-additivity in the latin square. *Biometrika*, 45, 69–73.

Cox, D. R. (1958b) *The Planning of Experiments*. New York: John Wiley.

Fisher, R. A. (1925) *Statistical Methods for Research Workers* (first ed.). Edinburgh: Oliver and Boyd.

Kempthorne, O. (1952) *The Design and Analysis of Experiments*. New York: John Wiley.

Neyman, J. (1923) On the application of probability theory to agricultural experiments. *Roczniki Nauk Rolniczvch*, X, 1–51. English translation: *Statistical Science* , 1990, 5, 465–480.

Ramirez, D. J., Yuen, S. D., Ramey, D. R., and Pasta, D. J. (1991a) Final report: Longitudinal study of structured-english immersion strategy, early-exit and late-exit transitional bilingual education programs for language-minority children, Volume I. Technical report, Aquirre International, San Mateo, Calif.

Ramirez, D. J., Pasta, D. J., Yuen, S. D., Billings, D. K., and Ramey, D. R. (1991b) Final report: Longitudinal study of structured-english immersion strategy, early-exit and late-exit transitional bilingual education programs for language-minority children, Volume II. Technical report, Aquirre International, San Mateo, Calif.

Rosenbaum, P., and Kreiger, A. (1990) Sensitivity of two-sample permutation inferences in observational studies. *Journal of the American Statistical Association*, 85, 493–498.

Rosenbaum, P. R. (1984) The consequences of adjustment for a concomitant variable that has been affected by the treatment. *Journal of the Royal Statistical Society Series A*, 147, 656–666.

Rosenbaum, P. R. (1986) Dropping out of high school in the United States: An observational study. *Journal of Educational Statistics*, 11, 207–224.

Rosenbaum, P. R. (1987) The role of a second control group in an observational study (with discussion). *Statistical Science*, 2, 292–316.

Rosenbaum, P. R. (1991) Discussing hidden bias in observational studies. *Annals of Internal Medicine*, 115(11), 901–905.

Rosenbaum, P. R., and Rubin, D. B. (1983) Assessing sensitivity to an unobserved binary covariate in an observational study with binary outcome. *Journal of the Royal Statistical Society, Series B*, 45, 212–218.

Rubin, D. B. (1974) Estimating the causal effects of treatments in randomized and nonrandomized studies. *Journal of Educational Psychology*, 66, 688–701.

Rubin, D. B. (1978) Bayesian inference for causal effects: The role of randomization. *Annals of Statistics*, 6, 34–58.

Rubin, D. B. (1984) William G. Cochran's contributions to the design, analysis, and evaluation of observational studies. In P. S. R. S. Rao and J. Sedransk, eds., *W. G Cochran's Impact on Statistics*, pp. 37–69. New York: Wiley.

U.S. Department of Education (1991) *The Condition of Bilingual Education in the Nation: A Report to the Congress and the President.* Office of the Secretary. Washington, D.C.: U.S. Department of Education.

Welch, B. L. (1937) On the z-test in randomized blocks and latin squares. *Biometrika*, 29, 21–52.

Wilk, M. B. (1955) The randomization analysis of a generalized randomized block design. *Biometrika*, 42, 70–79.

5

Lessons for the Future

This chapter addresses the issue of theory and its interplay with the statistical design of studies involving educational interventions. Building on experience in related areas of study and its review of the program in the Longitudinal and Immersion Studies, the panel has concluded that an explicit theory of bilingual education, including explicit objectives, is required to both motivate and structure the sensible statistical design of a study to evaluate alternative forms of bilingual education. Moreover, the development of a plan to evaluate an explicit theory must conform to the realities of the political and social setting of U.S. public education, as well as to the principles of sound experimental design and appropriate statistical analyses.

The panel believes strongly that without proper statistical designs most intervention studies are likely to fail. That is, they will be such that either the educational innovations will not achieve the desired objectives or the study will be insufficient to distinguish amongst innovations. The panel also believes that it is possible to overcome some shortcomings in design by relying on empirically supported theory. It is for this reason that the panel has focused on issues of underlying substantive theories and on related issues of statistical design of the two studies under review. The shortcomings of the Longitudinal and Immersion Studies are many, but they can be used to motivate the type of study that has a high probability of successfully demonstrating the value of particular forms of bilingual education.

SPECIFYING OBJECTIVES FOR BILINGUAL EDUCATION

The primary objectives of bilingual education for public schools in the United States remain controversial. In the absence of a well-defined set of program objectives, any research effort to assess "success" of programs will encounter problems and difficulties from the start.

For many, the primary objective of bilingual education is the development of English-language proficiency at the earliest possible age, to expedite the transition of language-minority limited-English-proficient (LM-LEP) students to classes for which English is the sole medium of communication. To meet this objective, instructional goals during early years of schooling would concentrate on the learning of English. Students, however, would be disadvantaged in subject-matter knowledge to the extent that they fall behind cohorts for whom English is their native language and who had already gained knowledge from classes taught in English.

An alternate, or perhaps concurrent, objective is to maintain equity of opportunity to learn subject-matter skills and knowledge, regardless of the students' facility in English at a given stage of development. This objective would seem to require subject-matter teaching in each child's native language until such time as sufficient proficiency in English allows the child to be an active learner in classes conducted in English. Still another objective may be the preservation of linguistic and cultural pluralism in U.S. society, and there may well be others.

From the perspective of students and their parents, the objectives may be somewhat different, and different objectives may be differentially important for children from different language groups. For example, some immigrant groups might encourage the early development of English-language facility for their children, while others might place greater importance on mastering their native language. Within a language community, different objectives may be favored for different subgroups of children, depending on the length of time since their arrival in this country, the values espoused by adults in the local community, or a variety of other factors.

It is imperative that objectives be agreed upon before assigning children to particular programs. Establishing program objectives is not a function of educational research, but, rather, must be accomplished as part of a political process. It is desirable that teachers, parents, and children be willing to accept program goals and subgoals, and that an instructional program then be oriented toward fulfilling those goals. Once objectives are set and programs to meet the objectives are in place, then criteria consistent with those objectives can be specified, and research designs to assess the relative success of alternative programs can be developed.

It is also important to have operational definitions of limited-English proficient (LEP) as well as fully English proficient (FEP). Without operational definitions, it is very difficult to quantify what the objectives of a bilingual education program are and just as difficult to decide if the objectives have been achieved. In the Immersion Study, the Foreign Service Institute oral proficiency test was used to measure the proficiency of teachers, but no measure of students' initial language proficiency was offered. The Foreign Service Institute oral proficiency test is inappropriate for young students, but other measures are available. Rather than leave the classification of LEP to local discretion, it is important that there be a uniform definition, at least within studies. In addition to descriptions of levels of English-language proficiency, future studies might also be enriched by descriptions of changes in language proficiency in the students' first language—in most cases, Spanish.

In addition to English-language proficiency, there are many other possible outcomes from bilingual education, such as the long-term impact of a program and its effect on students' attitude and motivation. The program that results in the "best" short-term effect may not prove to be the best in the long run. It is important to consider how one might measure long-term effects and the impact of a program on the subsequent motivation and attitude of students.

DEVELOPING INTERVENTIONS FROM THEORY

One of the fundamental difficulties that the panel encountered with its review of the Longitudinal and Immersion Studies was the absence of a careful description of an explicit theory for learning, either of language or school subject matter. This absence inevitably leaves a lean platform upon which to build data collection, analysis, and interpretation. As a result, the studies used vague and inconsistent methods to operationalize treatments, outcomes, and measurements. The problem was especially conspicuous in the Longitudinal Study, in which even the explanatory variables were inductively formulated without any explicit theory of learning or instruction. In the case of the Immersion Study, there is an explicit theory of treatment, but it is really a characterization of instructional strategies in terms of the amount of native-language involvement, and not tied, for example, to school and community contexts that might influence the choice and implementation of the programs.

In both studies, the key outcomes of interest were the students' English proficiency and their basic skills in reading and mathematics. What theory of education regards these outcomes as more important, to take an extreme example, than students self-esteem? Is there a theory that might explain how English proficiency is related to other desirable outcomes, such as access to instruction in general, access to instruction in a specific subject matter (for example, reading or mathematics) or motivation to learn? The panel had difficulty answering such questions on the basis of the material associated with the two studies it reviewed. Whatever structure a theory of bilingual education takes, it must address how the English and Spanish proficiency of students might introduce additional factors in the measurement of basic skills in reading and mathematics as a function of the language of the instrument (in the case of the two studies we reviewed, only English, since the Spanish achievement scores were not analyzed in the Immersion Study).

More generally, in such a theory, treatment, outcome, and measurement need much greater development and articulation. Otherwise, future studies of alternatives for bilingual education will not profit from the painful experiences of the Longitudinal and Immersion Studies. The rest of this section offers some guides to an array of theoretical components that might be of value for future studies.

The panel has attempted to construct an implicit theory around which the two studies were built; to do so we have read all of the available background information and planning documents, including the legislative language surrounding bilingual education, as well as the actual study reports. What comes through repeatedly is an implicit theory in which the treatment is almost exclusively concerned with the amount and duration of native-language instruction. One might ask, however, whether this dimension is really separable from community, demographic, and historical and other factors that form the context of a school. For example, is a program that fully utilizes native-language instruction (such as a Late-exit Program in the Immersion Study), implemented in a rural town on the U.S. border with Mexico, really comparable to one implemented in an urban immigrant community in Northern California? What are the sociological and educational theories that can explain the similarities and differences in the process by which a given treatment is implemented in different communities?

The idea that treatments are confounded with communities has become a major concern of the panel, especially for the Immersion Study. The rationale that Late-exit Programs could not be compared directly with other programs in the Immersion Study was justified in the face of glaring differences in the community contexts in which the programs existed. The panel questions the theoretical basis of that rationale. For example, there are several contextual community variables of possible interest that can be specified:

- the political base of language groups as reflected in bilingual education programs;
- rates of literacy or school involvement on the part of parents; and
- linguistic proficiency and ethnicity of the teachers in the programs.

There is a potentially infinite list of potential correlates of the treatment variables, but, in the absence of good theory, they are unavailable for empirical inquiry.

Equally critical is a theory of how the process or treatment affects the outcome. What is the theory of language proficiency (for example, how many dimensions does it have)? What is the theory of its acquisition (for example, rate, critical input, constraints, sources of group and individual variation)? And what is the relationship between the two languages that a student must master? Given natural variation in the amount and type of exposure to English depending on programs, what is the theory of language learning and the relationship between the two languages? For example, from the perspective of a theory of "time on task" as applied to second-language learning, it is interesting to note that the comparison of Immersion and Early-exit Programs provides rather disappointing evidence; those students who were exposed only to English performed significantly worse on English reading than those who were exposed to varying amounts of Spanish (see the discussion in Chapter 4, "Adjusting for Overt Biases"). If the effectiveness of instructional delivery might vary with the amount and duration of native-language instruction, what is the theory that relates language of instruction to learning of content? For example, from the viewpoint of student learning, what characterizes the relationship between a student's language proficiency and the student's ability to profit from instruction in English or Spanish? How involved are social and motivational factors in learning?

Perhaps more basic: What is the role of the teacher, other school personnel, and community in student learning? What defines language proficiency? Is it a purely cognitive construct devoid of the social circumstances of language use, or is it inseparable from sociolinguistic reality? Theories about student learning and expected outcomes offer the only way in which questions such as these might be systematically addressed—and answered by—research.

Issues surrounding the ways in which outcomes might be measured share parallels with the assessment of outcomes in most educational programs, such as, content, authenticity, level, and manner of assessment. In addition, there needs to be an articulation of how language proficiency interacts with measurement. Measurement involves the nature of language proficiency, which minimally needs to be distinguished between language for conversational and academic purposes. For example, superficial aspects of language proficiency, such as a non-native accent and clarity of speaking, may be influential in some performance-based assessment systems rather than in more traditional forms of assessment (for example, multiple choice tests). In contrast, variance in academic proficiency in English may take on increasing importance for measurements that require greater cognitive engagement of language, such as tests that require large amounts of reading or writing.

One clear lesson from the two studies the panel reviewed is the extent of variation across school sites and the fact that these variations are not randomly distributed. Thus, for example, in the Immersion Study, the safest inferences that could be drawn came from comparisons of programs in the same school. The differential effects of programs of the same bilingual education theory is perhaps best demonstrated in a study conducted under the auspices of the California State Department of Education, in which a theory of bilingual education was implemented in six different school sites. Samaniego and Eubank (1991, p. 13) concluded that:

> the effect of a given bilingual education initiative will vary with the environment in which it is implemented. In particular, a treatment which works well in one setting may fail in another, or may require nontrivial modifications if it is to be effective elsewhere.

The same sorts of warnings about generalizability can be made about the native languages of the students, whether their social setting is conducive for additive or subtractive bilingualism. In general it is very important to find out if a program *works* at all before becoming too concerned about the generalizability of the program results (see Cochran, 1965).

DESIGNING AND IMPLEMENTING EXPERIMENTS

The Applicability of Controlled Randomized Trials

In Chapter 2 the panel outlines a hierarchy of statistical designs for confirmatory evaluation studies, and it stresses the value of the randomized controlled experiments. The panel knows of few models of successful studies of bilingual educational approaches that have used a truly randomized experimental design. The are many reasons for this—including the practical difficulties investigators encounter when they try to adapt this evaluation strategy to the kinds of interventions at issue and the natural setting in which they must be implemented.

In other subject areas, such as evaluating the efficiency of alternative drug therapies in medicine, a controlled randomized trial is an effective evaluation strategy when three conditions are met:

1. the intervention is acute and, *a priori*, is expected to yield an acute outcome (produce a large effect);
2. the intervention acts rapidly, and the evaluation can be carried out over a short period of time.
3. the imposition of controls for the trial does not create an environment for the study that is substantially different from the environment in which the proposed therapy would be used on a routine basis.

Violations of 1. and 2. very frequently lead to lack of adherence to the study protocol; in medicine, much of the switching of patients among treatment regimens is driven by clinical patient management decisions that are both necessary (as judged by physicians) and in conflict with the original study design. This makes the evaluation of a therapy very problematic and reduces the chances of being able to provide conclusive results at the end of the study. Violation of 3. reflects strongly on generalizability of conclusions: in many instances it means that an artificial environment, having very little resemblance to the ultimate (clinical) setting and (patient) characteristics, is being used to evaluate a given intervention.

It is the panel's judgment that virtually all bilingual education interventions violate, at least to some extent, all three conditions. For example, a given teaching regimen in and of itself may have only a modest effect on improving test scores, presuming that test scores are the outcome to be measured. Thus, the experimental manipulations would violate 1. It is perfectly plausible, however, that a more complex treatment—for example, (Spanish literate parents) *and* (parents help children with homework) *and* (a given teaching regimen)—could have large effects, *but* only the third component can be manipulated in a randomized study. If an investigator designs a teaching regimen to operate over several years, this would represent a violation of 2. When 2. is violated, it is likely that uncontrolled and uncoordinated adaptive improvements will occur in the middle of a study when such improvements are judged by teachers and principals to be desirable. This situation makes it extremely difficult to generalize study results because of a lack of precision about what the treatments are and the consequent inability to duplicate them. Moreover, different adaptations are likely to occur at different sites, creating unplanned variations in treatments. Finally, if school rules, class composition, and a variety of other structural changes at the school level are imposed for purposes of an evaluation study without any intent of permanence of the arrangements, condition 3. would be violated.

For the evaluation of bilingual education treatments, the panel believes that multiple highly focused studies are likely to be much more informative than a single large study. Since discovery of candidates for a potentially successful treatment is an integral part of the bilingual education research agenda, multiple studies that vary across intervention and environment are more likely to both uncover potential winners and afford insight into how interventions and setting interact.

A problem with such a series of studies, whether the sampling of sites is random or not, is the introduction of at least three new components of variation: (1) variations on the intervention over space and time, (2) the interaction of intervention with environment, and (3) variation in the magnitude of measurement error across the studies. In agricultural experiments, Yates and Cochran (1938) note these difficulties, and we discuss them below.

Formal statistical methods for combining information across experiments have a long history in the physical and agricultural sciences. More recently, meta-analyses have been carried out in education, psychology, medicine and other social science settings. More elaborate statistical modeling for combining evidence across sites or studies was used by DuMouchel and Harris (1983) for combining evidence from cancer experiments and by Mason, Wong, and Entwisle (1984) for a comparative analysis of fertility patterns across 30 developing countries. Mosteller and Tukey (1982, 1984) treat combining evidence from multiple sources more generally; see also Wachter and Straf (1990).

Meta-analytic techniques were originally planned for use in the analysis of the longitudinal study. The research design overview (Development Associates, 1984a) states:

> [the] mere presence of common ... instruments does not guarantee that they are suitable for directly combining across several sites into a single analysis. [Objectively derived measures such as] test scores ... normally *are* combinable across sites ... However, subjectively determined ratings ... normally are *not* suitable for across-site combination [because between site variability, and because raters differ between sites and] rater-specific biases are almost certain to distort the picture ... But meta-analytic techniques *will* enable us to combine *conclusions* drawn from ratings at different sites.

We believe this conclusion is warranted in bilingual research and we recommend that multiple studies be combined in this way. Such studies are, however, best carried out independently, perhaps with some coordination to ensure that similar measures are taken across sites. A single large study such as the Longitudinal Study is likely to fail to account adequately for the special factors affecting each of the sites.

Evolutionary Study Design

In addition to combining information across different studies as described above, it is useful to plan for sequential accumulation of knowledge. One such experimental program is "evolutionary operation" (EVOP)—see Box and Draper (1969, 1987). EVOP uses the results of a subexperiment both to check model assumptions and to suggest the most efficient way to improve the model for the follow-on subexperiment. Similar evolutionary processes have been used in educational research under the label of "formative evaluation".

For bilingual education research, Tharp and Gallimore (1979) provide a model for program development at evaluation that has great potential. They describe systematic strategies for adaptive study design which should be the basis for sequential discovery of causal mechanisms (treatments) and then evaluation in bilingual education interventions. Tharp and Gallimore (1979) applied their sequential approach, which they call succession evaluation, to the study of educational alternatives for underachieving Hawaiian native children. They used a much smaller scale than that typically used in a large EVOP industrial experiment, and they used less formal and less complicated statistical methods. Letting data from one phase of a study inform choices of succeeding phases has, however, led to the development of educational programs that appear to work.

Table 5–1, taken from Tharp and Gallimore (1979), outlines the succession evaluation model. Their first steps in developing a program are likely to be more qualitative and subjective, involving the development of theoretical questions, the consideration of qualitative data to understand the phenomenon or program under study, analysis of previous research, and clarification of values. At this stage they ask such questions as, "Does this idea make sense?" and "Is it generalizable?"

Moving from planning to experimentation occurs at step 3, which is still at the qualitative and subjective level. Step 4 tests the program in an experimental setting, possibly with successive interactions to improve the program and testing new elements. The final step of one complete cycle of program development is testing the full-scale program. The evaluation at this step may lead to a recycling to step 1 to develop new or improve existing program elements.

This paradigm has also been suggested for research in other areas, such as the rehabilitation of criminal offenders (National Research Council, 1981) and, in the panels' view, shows great potential for bilingual education research.

There is an inevitable tension between possible contamination among units and the desire to maintain comparability between treatment and control groups. For example, consider an experiment that used "advertising" as a treatment. The treatment might be applied to a specific neighborhood of a city with the control neighborhood (chosen for comparability) being in close geographic proximity.

TABLE 5–1   An Evaluation Succession for Program Research and Development

Stages	Stages in Program Element Development	Ways of Knowing	Validity Concerns	Selection Process
	Step 1. Initial selection values, theories, goals, and objectives	Qualitative/personal	Construct and External	Does the idea have potential?
1	Step 2. Treatment, independent variable formation	Experimentation: true or quasi	External-internal or internal-external	Are the relationships of enough magnitude?
2	Step 3. Decision point: review, evaluate, translate; proceed, recycle	Qualitative/personal	Construct and External	Can treatments/independent variables be translated into stable, program element(s)?
3	Step 4. Program element formation	Experimentation: true or quasi	External-internal	Does it work in the setting employed?
	Step 5. Decision point: review, evaluate, proceed, recycle	Qualitative/personal	Constructive and external	Is it worth further work
	Step 6. Program element implementation	Data guidance	External-internal	Can it be improved with tinkering?
	Step 7. Decision point review, evaluate, proceed	Qualitative/personal	Construct and external	When and if in or out of the program?
	Step 8. Full-scale program element operation	Program evaluation	Internal and conclusion, statistical	Does the program element, with other elements in association, bring benefit?

SOURCE: Taken from Tharp and Gallimore (1979)

Knowledge of the advertising campaign in the treatment neighborhood could readily be transmitted to the control neighborhood, thereby converting it into a treatment neighborhood. For a classic example of this phenomenon, see Freedman and Takeshita (1969), which gives a superb discussion of the design and analysis of a randomized advertising experiment on behalf of birth control strategies.

In many evaluation studies, the responses to treatments are often found to vary dramatically in what is referred to as "a change from one environment to another." This finding is frequently viewed as a negative finding; however, it can also be thought of as a clue to the definition of a more complex cause in which environmental conditions (that is, a profile of environmental attributes) define part of the cause. Taking this point of view changes the way one thinks about the definition of "intervention": indeed this interaction is usually viewed as an treatment-by-environment interaction. The panel believes, however, that it may be productive to think of an evaluation study in which "treatment," as usually constituted, corresponds to the part of a complex cause that can be manipulated, while the "environment" component of the complex cause corresponds to the part that can only be studied observationally. If this point of view is adopted, then program evaluation consists of a mixture of experimental and observational studies. As an example of this view for bilingual education evaluation, a candidate cause for successful performance on tests is (Spanish-literate parents) *and* (parents help children with homework) *and* (late-exit language program). One can manipulate the language program but must find natural settings (communities) to see variation in (Spanish literate parents) and (parents help children with homework).

REFERENCES

Box, G. E. P., and Draper, N. R. (1969) *Evolutionary Operation: A Statistical Method for Process Improvement*. New York: John Wiley.

Box, G. E. P., and Draper, N. R. (1987) *Empirical Model-building and Response Surfaces*. New York: John Wiley.

Cochran, W. G. (1965) The planning of observational studies of human populations (with discussion). *Journal of the Royal Statistical Society, Series A*, 128, 124–135.

Development Associates (1984) The descriptive phase report of the national longitudinal study of the effectiveness of services for LMLEP students. Technical report, Development Associates Inc., Arlington, Va.

DuMouchel, W. H., and Harris, J. E. (1983) Bayes methods for combining the results of cancer studies in humans and other species (with discussion). *Journal of the American Statistical Association*, 78, 293–308.

Freedman, R., and Takeshita, J. (1969) *Family Planning in Taiwan: An Experiment in Social Change*. Princeton, N.J.: Princeton University Press.

Mason, W. M., Wong, G. Y., and Entwisle, B. (1984) Contextual analysis through the multilevel linear model. In S. Leinhardt, ed., *Sociological Methodology 1984*, pp. 72–103. Washington, D.C.: American Sociological Association.

Mosteller, F., and Tukey, J. W. (1982) Combination of results of stated precision: I. the optimistic case. *Utilitas Mathematica*, 21, 155–178.

Mosteller, F., and Tukey, J. W. (1984) combination of results of stated precision: II. a more realistic case. In P. S. R. S. Rao and J. Sedransk, eds., *W. G. Cochran's Impact on Statistics*, pp. 223–252. New York: John Wiley.

National Research Council (1981) *New Directions in the Rehabilitation of Criminal Offenders*. Panel on Research on Rehabilitative Techniques, Committee on Research on Law Enforcement and the Administration of Justice, Commission on Behavioral and Social Sciences and Education, National Research Council. Washington, D.C.: National Academy Press.

Samaniego, F. J., and Eubank, L. A. (1991) A statistical analysis of California's case study project in bilingual education. Technical Report 208, Division of Statistics, University of California, Davis.

Tharp, R., and Gallimore, R. (1979) The ecology of program research and evaluation: A model of succession evaluation. In L. Sechrest, M. Philips, R. Redner, and S. West, eds., *Evaluation Studies Review Annual: 4*. Beverly Hills, Calif.: Sage Publications.

Wachter, K. W., and Straf, M. L., eds. (1990) *The Future of Meta-Analysis*. Committee on National Statistics, Commission on Behavioral and Social Sciences and Education, National Research Council. New York: Russell Sage Foundation.

Yates, F., and Cochran, W. G. (1938) The analysis of groups of experiments. *The Journal of Agricultural Science*, XXVIII(IV), 556–580.

6

Conclusions and Recommendations

In this chapter we present first our summaries of the reports of the Immersion and Longitudinal Studies and our overall conclusions about the studies. In the second part of this chapter we present specific conclusions and recommendations about the Longitudinal and Immersion Studies and our general conclusions and recommendations regarding future studies on bilingual education.

SUMMARIES

The Longitudinal Study

The Longitudinal Study consisted of two phases. The first phase described the range of services provided to language-minority limited-English-proficient (LM-LEP) students in the United States; it was used to estimate the number of children in grades K–6 receiving special language-related services. The second phase was a 3-year longitudinal component to evaluate the effectiveness of different types of educational services provided to LM-LEP students. The longitudinal component itself consisted of two parts, a baseline survey and a series of follow-up studies in the subsequent years.

The initial sample design and survey methodology of the descriptive component are appropriate for making inferences that describe the U.S. population. For the longitudinal component, the method of subsampling makes it highly questionable if such inferences are possible. Since the data were used primarily for developing models, this drawback does not of itself invalidate the results of the analyses.

The large extent of missing data and measurement error in the Longitudinal Study severely limits the usefulness of the study data. This, and the very large number of variables measured, made the original plans for analysis unworkable. A distinct and rather ad hoc procedure was subsequently used for analysis, and it produced inconclusive results.

The use of variables to characterize treatment characteristics, rather than classifying programs into different explicit types (as originally envisaged in the design), means that it is difficult or impossible to separate genuine treatment effects from the effects of other factors. This in turn means that the findings from the study are very difficult to generalize to a wider population.

The data collected, despite the limitations noted, are likely to be useful in addressing some research questions, although these questions were not central to the objectives of the study. The analyses will likely take the form of describing, but not evaluating, bilingual education programs: that is, what programs existed in the United States at the time of the Longitudinal Study. In particular, data from the the descriptive component constitute a sound database for such descriptive, nonevaluative research. The panel does not believe that further analyses of data from the study can provide the kinds of evaluation of the effectiveness of bilingual education programs that were originally envisaged.

The Immersion Study

The Immersion Study was designed to compare the relative effectiveness of three strategies for educating children at the elementary school level:

- structured English Immersion Program (all instruction in English, lasting 2–3 years);
- Early-exit Program of transitional bilingual education (both languages used in instruction, but subject-matter content taught in English; instruction lasted 2–3 years); and
- Late-exit Program of transitional bilingual education (both languages used in instruction, including content areas; instruction lasted 5–6 years).

Although the study's final report claims that the three programs represent three distinct instructional models, the findings indicate that the programs were not that distinct. They were essentially different versions of the same treatment; Immersion and Early-exit Programs were in some instances indistinguishable from one another.

In addition, all three program settings were characterized by rote-like instruction directed by teachers, in which student language use was minimal. Given the unexceptional nature of the instruction, the question arises as to whether there were any reasonable grounds for anticipating a substantial educational effect, regardless of language of instruction.

Several features about the study design and analyses make it difficult to interpret the Immersion Study. Outcomes and covariates are not always distinguished from one another. Thus, controls for intermediate outcomes are not routinely present and the measurement of treatment (program) effects may be distorted. Even if outcomes are not used as covariates, the need for controls remains. For cohorts of students first observed after entry into the school system, there were few covariates, and key baseline measurements were often absent. It is not clear whether differences in many measured variables are indicators of pre-existing student characteristics or if they reflect prior exposure to one program or another.

There are strong suggestions of such pre-existing differences among the students exposed to each type of program, which parallel differences in students across schools and school districts and the nonrandom allocation of programs to districts and schools. For example, students in Late-exit Programs were from far more economically disadvantaged backgrounds than those in either Immersion or Early-exit Programs. On the other hand, the parents of the students in Late-exit Programs were as likely as parents of students in other programs to receive English-language newspapers and twice as likely to receive Spanish-language newspapers—perhaps an indication of Spanish literacy. Other characteristics of the sites of Late-exit Programs make them potentially important sites for future studies. For example, the family income of students in Late-exit Programs was by far the lowest in the study, but these families monitored completion of homework considerably more than the families at the other sites. Furthermore, children at the sites of Late-exit Programs scored at or above the norm in standardized tests, suggesting a possible relationship between the use of Spanish for instruction, Spanish literacy in the home, parental involvement in homework, and student achievement.

Notwithstanding these general problems in the Immersion Study, there is one conclusions for which the panel finds reasonably compelling and credible analyses: the difference between students in Immersion and in Early-exit Programs at kindergarten and grade 1. Early-exit Programs appear to be more successful in reading and because of the early age of these children, concerns about pre-observation treatment effects are not severe. By grades 1–3, however, differences in student achievement by program are not easily distinguished from possible differences in where the students started. Thus, conclusions from analyses at these grades are tenuous.

The final report of the Immersion Study notes that school effects are not directly separable from program effects; the panel concurs with this conclusion. In addition, Late-exit Programs were rare and were found in districts without any other program type. Given the presence of substantial differences in school districts, it is virtually impossible to compare Late-exit with either Early-exit or Immersion Programs. We do not know how effective Late-exit Programs were.

THE PANEL'S CONCLUSIONS AND RECOMMENDATIONS

Conclusions Related to the Longitudinal and Immersion Studies

- *The formal designs of the the Longitudinal and Immersion Studies were ill-suited to answer the important policy questions that appear to have motivated them.*

The studies lacked a firm conceptual grounding and did not articulate specific objectives. The objectives that were stated were often conflicting or unrealizable. There was a misfit between the program objectives and the program implementation.

- *Execution and interpretation of these studies—especially the Longitudinal Study—was hampered by a lack of documentation regarding (a) objectives, (b) operationalization of conceptual details, (c) actual procedures followed, and (d) changes in all of the above.*

For example, the objectives of the Longitudinal Study changed substantially between the year 1 report on data collection and the subsequent request for proposal (RFP) for data analysis. In the Immersion Study, the RFP specified an evaluation of only two interventions (Immersion and Early-exit Programs); the contract was later amended to involve a third treatment (Late-exit Program). Absence of adequate documentation is in part a function of the complexity of the studies and their duration, but it appears to have been exacerbated by shifts in the directives from the contract administrators as well as the mid-project changes of contractors.

- *Because of the poor articulation of study goals and the lack of fit between the discernible goals and the research design, it is unlikely that additional statistical analyses of these data will yield results central to the policy question to which these studies were originally addressed.*

This conclusion does not mean, however, that the data collected are uniformly of no value. The data may prove valuable to those requiring background information for the planning of new programs and studies.

- *Both the Longitudinal and Immersion Studies suffered from excessive attention to the use of elaborate statistical methods intended to overcome the shortcomings in the research designs.*

Methods of statistical analysis cannot repair failures in the conceptualization, design, and implementation of studies. Techniques such as path analysis (as planned for and abortively implemented in the Longitudinal Study) and Trajectory Analysis of Matched Percentiles (TAMP) (as implemented in the Immersion Study) provide limited insight. The assumptions inherent in them at best finesse and at worst obfuscate issues that needed to have been dealt with explicitly in the study design and attendant analysis.

- *The absence of clear findings in the Longitudinal and Immersion Studies that distinguish among the effects of treatments and programs relating to bilingual education does not warrant conclusions regarding differences in program effects, in any direction.*

The studies do not license the conclusion that any one type of program is superior to any other nor that the programs are equally effective. Even if one of the programs was definitively superior, the studies as planned and executed could well have failed to find the effect.

- *Taking fully into account the limitations of the two studies, the panel still sees the elements of positive relationships that are consistent with empirical results from other studies and that support the theory underlying native-language instruction in bilingual education.*

Most noteworthy is convergence of the studies in suggesting, under certain conditions, the importance of primary-language instruction in second-language achievement in language arts and mathematics.

Specific Recommendations for the Longitudinal and Immersion Studies

In the light of the foregoing conclusions, the panel makes the following specific recommendations for further analysis and examination of the data from the Longitudinal and Immersion Studies.

- *The panel recommends that the U.S. Department of Education not seek to fund any specific additional analyses of the data from the Longitudinal or Immersion Studies.*

The panel was asked by the Department of Education to recommend possible additional analyses that would be of value in addressing the objectives of the studies. In Chapters 3 and 4 of this report the panel points to some specific analyses which could have been performed. *It is the panel's judgment, however, that additional analyses are unlikely to change its assessment of the conclusions that can be drawn from the studies.*

- *The panel recommends that the data and associated documentation from both the Longitudinal and Immersion Studies be archived and made publicly available.*

The data from both studies were made available to the panel, but attempts by the panel to use the data were unsuccessful.

- *Given the diversity between study sites that made adequate comparisons impossible, the panel recommends more focused and theoretically driven studies to analyze the interaction of different instructional approaches in bilingual education contexts of specific community characteristics.*

Some Desiderata Regarding Evaluation Studies in Bilingual Education

Throughout this report the panel addresses issues of research design in various ways and discusses the role of discovery and confirmatory studies. We summarize here some broad themes about the design of such studies that are worthy of special attention:

- A study without clear, focused goals will almost certainly fail.
- Determining effective programs requires at least three tasks. First, an attempt must be made to identify features of programs that may be important. This first task is usually best achieved in *exploratory or qualitative studies* by comparing existing programs. The second task is to *develop competing*

theories leading to sharply distinct proposals for programs. The third task is to create these new programs to specifications and assess their effectiveness in several tightly controlled and conclusive *comparative studies*. An attempt to combine all three tasks in a single comprehensive study is likely to fail.

- Program effects will often be small in comparison to differences among communities and among demographic and socioeconomic groups. Therefore, comparative studies must compare programs in the same communities and demographic and socioeconomic groups. Program effects may vary from one community to another. Therefore, several comparative studies in different communities are needed. In comparative studies, comparability of students in different programs is more important than having students who are representative of the nation as a whole.

- Elaborate analytic methods will not salvage poor design or implementation of a study. Elaborate statistical methods are for the analysis of data collected in well-implemented, well-designed studies. Care in design and implementation will be rewarded with useful and clear study conclusions.

- Large quantities of missing data may render a study valueless. Active steps must be taken to limit missing data and to evaluate its impact.

- A publicly funded research study requires clear documentation of decisions about study design and analysis plans, including changes that evolve as the study progresses. A well-documented, publicly accessible archived database should be made available from any publicly funded study.

- The size and structure of both discovery and confirmatory studies needs to be linked to objectives that can be realized. Overly ambitious large-scale studies implemented in broad national populations, such as the Longitudinal and Immersion Studies, inevitably are difficult to control, even if the interventions and their implementation are well understood. Discovery studies of bilingual education interventions must begin on a small scale. For confirmatory studies, small-scale experiments or quasi-experiments are also more timely and informative than large-scale studies, especially if their design controls for potentially confounding factors.

Appendix A

Bilingual Education in the United States

A BRIEF HISTORY

We excerpt here from U.S. Department of Education (1991), to provide a long-range context for the current controversies about bilingual education:

Although Federal involvement with bilingual education in the United States began with the passage of the Bilingual Education Act of 1968, an amendment to Title VII of the Elementary and Secondary Education Act (ESEA) of 1965, it has its roots in early nineteenth-century America.

In the public schools of a number of states between 1839 and 1880, including Ohio, Louisiana, and New Mexico, German, French and Spanish were used for instruction. Between 1880 and 1917, German-English bilingual schools, in which both languages were used for instruction, operated in Ohio, Minnesota, and Maryland. In several other states, German was included in the curriculum as a subject rather than as a means of instruction. The same is true for Norwegian, Italian, Czech, Dutch, and Polish.[1]

In private schools, mostly parochial, German-English bilingual education flourished throughout the United States before 1800. Also during this period, many French schools were established in the northeastern United States (precursors of the modern-day Lyçée Français found in New York City, for example), and Scandinavian and Dutch schools were formed in the Midwest. It should be noted that many of these institutions were not actually bilingual schools but rather non-English schools that taught English as a subject in the curriculum. After 1880, the number of private schools offering instruction in other languages proliferated and included many, still in existence, for Japanese and Chinese children on the West Coast.

---

[1] Texas Education Agency, *Report on Bilingual Education*, 1990

Contrary to the widely accepted myth that earlier immigrant groups managed without special programs, most immigrant children who entered schools were more likely to sink than swim in English-only language classrooms. In 1908, for example, just 13 percent of the twelve-year-olds enrolled in New York public schools, and whose parents were foreign-born, went on to high school, compared with 32 percent of white children whose parents were native-born, see Crawford (1989). Some immigrants with limited English skills and no formal education were able to succeed because the economy, with its industrial and agricultural base, relied on uneducated and unskilled labor.

From 1919 to 1950, American education turned away from the use of languages other than English for instruction in both the public and the private schools. This period in American history was marked by intense nativism. Public sentiment toward many foreign nationals and immigrants was not generally favorable. Instruction became increasingly concentrated in English to the exclusion of other languages. These changes particularly affected speakers of German, the group that had fostered bilingual education most extensively prior to the First World War. In many states, laws governing education resulted in school systems in which generations of children were scorned and punished for speaking languages other than English in school.

One of the most important changes to occur in American society during the twentieth century was the transformation from an economy that relied on large numbers of unskilled workers to one that demanded highly trained workers. English literacy skills became virtually indispensable for increased participation in the labor force, although immigrants with no English skills or formal education could still find work in agricultural or service sector jobs in rural areas, cities and suburbs.

In a memorandum dated May 25, 1970, the Office for Civil Rights in the former Department of Health, Education, and Welfare advised school districts of their responsibility to provide special language services to limited English proficient students under Title VI of the Civil Rights Act of 1964. The U.S. Supreme Court upheld this requirement in its 1974 decision in *Lau v. Nichols*. Since then the Office for Civil Rights has reviewed and approved special language services programs in hundreds of school districts nationwide. In addition, in its recently issued National Enforcement Strategy, the Office for Civil Rights made the provision of equal educational opportunities for national origin minority and American Indian students who are limited English proficient a priority issue for .

The following definitions and classifications used in bilingual education are also take from U.S. Department of Education (1991):

Methods to Identify Limited-English-Proficient Students

Within the parameters of state statutes and regulations, school districts use their own criteria for identifying LEP students. Current methods used by school districts generally include a combination of the following:

1. Teacher information or referral;
2. Parent information;
3. Home language surveys to gather information on students' language and background;
4. Evaluation of student records;

5. Assessment of achievement level — a formal or informal procedure to determine students' levels of achievement in various academic subjects; and

6. Language assessment tests — a formal or informal procedure to determine a student's level of English proficiency.

According to the Bilingual Education Act, the terms limited "English proficiency" and "limited "English proficient" refer to: "[A] individuals who were not born in the United States or whose native language is a language other than English; "[B] individuals who come from environments where a language other than English is dominant; and "[C] individuals who are American Indian and Alaska Natives and who come from environments where a language other than English has had a significant impact on their level of English language proficiency; and who, by reason thereof, have sufficient difficulty speaking, reading, writing, or understanding the English language to deny such individuals the opportunity to learn successfully in classrooms where the language of instruction is English or to participate fully in society. 20 U.S.C. 3283 (a)(1).

The Title VII legislation offers a broad definition of LEP and allows for a variety of groups, all of whom must meet the statutory definition of LEP. State laws establish a variety of instructional methods.

Many states use multiple methods for student identification. For example, California and Colorado use language assessment, achievement and criterion referenced tests, home language surveys, and oral language assessments. New York relies on language assessment tests and home language surveys.

Number and Distribution of Limited-English-Proficient Students Across the States

In an effort to estimate the number of limited English proficient children in the United States, the Department [of Education] commissioned the Bureau of the Census to conduct the English Language Proficiency Survey in the early 1980's. This survey entailed the administration of tests to determine the English language proficiency of a nationally representative sample of language minority children. Based on an extensive analysis of these data, the Department estimated that as of January 1986, between 1.2 million and 1.7 million children aged 5-17 lived in language minority households in the fifty states and the District of Columbia, made substantial use of a language other than English, and scored at or below the twentieth percentile on a measure of English language proficiency.

In a more recent estimate, the state education agencies receiving Title VII funding reported in school year 1989-90 a count of about 2.2 million limited English proficient students, including 227,000 limited English proficient students in Puerto Rico and the outlying territories and associated republics.

The population of LEP students has not remained constant throughout the United States. In 1989-90, California reported in increase of 118,972 LEP students, which represents an increase of 14 percent between school years. Unexpectedly, the greatest reported percentage increases in LEP students occurred in the Midwest: 38 percent in Montana; 46 percent in Oklahoma; 39 percent in South Dakota; and the 36 percent in North Dakota. In the East, Delaware reported a 41 percent increase. Several states reported only slight

TABLE A–1   Methods Used By Participating States and Territories To Determine LEP Status, FY 1989

Methods Used	States Reporting Use of Method	Number of States
1. Language Assessment Tests	AK, AS, AZ, CA, CO, CT, CN,MI, DC, DE, GA, GU, HI, IA, ID, IL, IN, KS, LA, MD, MI, MN, MO, MS, MT, NC, ND, NE, NH, NJ, NM, NV, NY, OH, OK, OR, PALAU, PR, RI, SD, TN, TX, UT, VI, VT, WA, WI	47
2. Achievement and Criterion-Referenced Tests	AK, CO, CT, DC, DE, GU, LA, ID, IN, KS, LA, MD, MI, MN, MO, MS, MT, NC, ND, NM, NV, OH, OK, PALAU, PR, RI, SD, TN, TX, UT, VI,WI, WY	39
3. Teacher/Tutor Observation/Referral	AS, CO, CT, DC, DE, GU, IA, ID, IN, KS KY, LA, MA, MD, MI, MN, MO, MS, MT, NC, ND, NH, NV, OH, SD, TN, VI, WI, WY	30
4. Home Language Survey/Enrollment Form	AS, AZ, CA, CO, CT, CN,MI, DC, GU, HI, IL MD, MI, NE, NH, NJ, ND, NM, OH, PALAU, RI, SD, TN, TX, VI, VT, WY	27
5. Oral Language Assessment/Interview/ Speech Test	AS, AZ, CA, CO, CT, DC, GU, HI, IL, MD, MI, MN, MS, MT, ND, NM, OK, SD, TX, VI, WA, WI, WY	25
6. Parent Information/ Recommendations	AK, AS, CO, DE, IA, ID, KS, KY, LA, MI, MN, MS, MT, NH, NC, ND, NE, NV, OH, OK, TN, VI, WI,	24
7. Grades	CT, DE, IN, KS, LA, MI, MN, MS, MT, NC, ND, PALAU, TN, VI, WI,	15
8. Informal Assessment/ Information	DE, IN, KS, KY, MD, MI, MN, MS, NC,ND, NV, VT, VI, WI	14
9. Students Comprehensive Records	AS, IA, IN, KS, LA, MI, MN, MS, MT, NC, ND, NV, SD	13
10. Committee/School Consultation Team	CN,MI, IN, KS, LA, MI, MN, MS, ND, NV, SD,	10
11. LEA Survey Form	AS, FL, ME, NH, NJ, OH	6
12. Locally Developed Tests	AZ, MD, MO, NJ, PALAU, VI	6
13. State Management Information Systems	FL, GA, ME	3
14. Grade Retention/ Deficiency	KS	1
15. School Recommendation	NE	1

SOURCE: "Title VII SEA Data Report for FY 1989," OBEMLA, U.S. Department of Education, May 1991.

increases in their LEP populations; among these were Hawaii, Mississippi, and New York.

Two states reported notable decreases in LEP populations between school years 1988-89 and 1989-90: 30 percent in Louisiana, 28 percent in Tennessee. Differences in criteria utilized in identifying LEP students, and improved counting procedures, may account for some of the dramatic changes, but there may be additional causes. These states may have fewer new LEP students enrolling in schools and existing LEP students may be learning English.

There is considerable variation among the states in terms of the proportion of LEP students among their overall student populations as reported for school year 1989-90. California reported 16 percent of its student population as LEP, New Mexico reported 19 percent, and Texas reported 9 percent. A number of states reported less than 1 percent.

CHRONOLOGY OF IMPORTANT EVENTS IN BILINGUAL EDUCATION POLICY

1968 Title VII of the Elementary and Secondary Education Act provided funds for staff and materials development as well as parent involvement for students with limited English skills. There was no requirement for schools to use non-English language. The law was specified for students who are both poor and "educationally disadvantaged because of their inability to speak English." Signed on Jan. 2, 1968, by Johnson.

1971 (November) Massachusetts passed the Transitional Bilingual Education Act promoting transitional bilingual education in school districts with 20 or more students from same language background; followed by Alaska and California (1972); Arizona, Illinois, New Mexico, and Texas (1973); Michigan, New York, and Rhode Island (1974); Colorado, Louisiana, New Jersey, and Wisconsin (1975); Indiana (1976), Connecticut, Maine, Minnesota, and Utah (1977); and Iowa, Kansas, Oregon, and Washington (1979).

1974 (January) *Lau* v. *Nichols* decision based on Title VI of the Civil Rights Act. The Supreme Court ruled that "there is no equality of treatment merely by providing students with the same facilities, textbooks, teachers, and curriculum; for students who do not understand English are effectively foreclosed from any meaningful education." Regarding remedies the Court ruled that "no specific remedy is urged upon us. Teaching English to the students of Chinese ancestry who do not speak the language is one choice. Giving instructions to this group in Chinese is another. There may be others. Petitioners ask only that the Board of Education be directed to apply its expertise to the problem and rectify the situation."

1974 Re-authorization of Bilingual Education Act. The poverty criterion was dropped, and the act also required schools to include instruction in native language and culture.

1975 Lau remedies issued by the Commissioner of Education, Bell, on August 11. These remedies went beyond the Lau decision and required that bilingual education must be provided. These remedies were drafted and circulated without public comment and were not equivalent to Federal regulations.

1978 AIR study, *Evaluation of the Impact of ESEA Title VII Spanish/English Bilingual Education Program*, released in January.

1978 Reauthorization of Bilingual Education Act. Mandated data collection and coordination of these activities by different agencies of the Office of Education (Part C).

1979 *Proposed Research Plan for Bilingual Education* issued by the Education Division, U.S. Department of Health, Education, and Welfare, in response to a request from Congress.

1979 Study of Significant Bilingual Instructional Features started, planned for 4 years (fiscal years 1979–1982).

1980 The Department of Education is created, and the Office of Bilingual Education is expanded to the Office of Bilingual Education and Minority Languages Affairs (OBEMLA).

1980 The Lau regulations were proposed by Carter administration on August 5, to mandate bilingual education in schools with at least 25 LEP students from same language group in K-8. The proposed regulations were withdrawn by the Reagan administration (Bell) on Feb. 2, 1981, which called them "harsh, inflexible, burdensome, unworkable, and incredibly costly," and criticized native language instruction as "an intrusion on state and local responsibility .... We will protect the rights of children who do not speak English well, but we will do so by permitting school districts to use any way that has proven to be successful" (Crawford, 1989, page 43).

1981 *Castañeda* v. *Pickard*. The Court of Appeals interpreted Equal Education Opportunities Act of 1974 statement of "appropriate action" as requiring the meeting of three criteria: (1) it must be based on a "sound educational theory;" (2) it must be "implemented effectively" with adequate resources and personnel, and (3) after a trial period, it must be evaluated as effective in overcoming language handicaps (Crawford, 1989, page 47).

1981 (September) The Baker and de Kanter internal OPBE document, "Effectiveness of Bilingual Education: A Review of the Literature," was circulated.

1982 The RFP for National Longitudinal Evaluation of the Effectiveness of Services for Language-Minority Limited-English-Proficient Students was issued by Department of Education; closing date Sept. 7.

1983 "Longitudinal Study of Immersion and Dual Language Instructional Programs for Language Minority Children" begun 12/15/83 through 12/15/88; fiscal year 1983 funds of $1,400,000.

1983 "National Longitudinal Evaluation of the Effectiveness of Services to Language Minority, LEP Students" begun 9/20/83 through 9/88; fiscal year 1983 funds of $1,505,000.

1984 Reauthorization of Bilingual Education Act reserved 4–10 percent of total appropriations for Special Alternative Instructional Programs that do not require instruction in native language. National Advisory Council for Bilingual Education eliminated.

1985 The Secretary of Education, William Bennett, launched an initiative to remove the 4 percent cap for Special Alternative Instructional Programs and advocated greater flexibility and local control (Sept. 26).

1987 The GAO study that criticized the claims of the Department of Education was released with responses from Chester Finn representing the department's position.

1988 Reauthorization of Bilingual Education Act; up to 25 percent of funds were made available for Special Alternative Instructional Programs.

Appendix B

Trajectory Analysis of
Matched Percentiles

This appendix describes and provides a short discussion of a graphical methodology called trajectory analysis of matched percentiles (TAMP) and its limitations. Volume 2 of the final report of the Immersion Study (Ramirez et al., 1991b) makes extensive use of TAMP graphs. TAMP was proposed by Braun (1988) and is based in part on earlier work of Braun and Holland (1982). The 1988 paper by Braun is quite clear and does an excellent job of describing the underlying graphical tool.

TAMP graphs are a simple tool for comparing change (or growth) from cross-sectional data. Consider two populations of students that each take two standardized tests. Suppose one is interested in the differences in improvement for the two populations. When the data consist of a pair of scores for each student, there are many multivariate techniques—from simple *t*-tests to discriminant analysis and clustering—that might be used to compare the populations. Sometimes one may only have the marginal scores (that is, the scores for each population on each test), without knowing the exact pair of scores that each individual student has achieved. This is especially common in longitudinal studies in schools: in many cases there may be only a small percentage of students who stay in the same school from year to year so the number of students with complete longitudinal records becomes very small. In other words, one may have the marginal distribution of scores for a cohort (for example, class of students) at two different times, but there may be very few students who are members of the cohort at both times. This is especially the case in migrant communities and in early school years—precisely the situations for which careful measurement is most important. Even when one knows the pair of scores for most students, it may be convenient to use only the marginal scores. A TAMP graph uses just this cross-sectional, or marginal, information to provide a comparison of the improvement in the two populations. The TAMP methodology does not provide a definitive analysis of data, but it is a useful exploratory and descriptive tool.

A TAMP graph for comparing N populations on two tests is a line graph with N lines on it. Each line (one for each population) is a Q-Q probability plot (Gnanadesikan, 1977) comparing the marginal distribution on the second test (plotted on the vertical axis) with the marginal distribution on the first test (plotted on the horizontal axis). If the marginal distribution of scores on the two test is the same, then the Q-Q plot will be straight lines—deviations from linearity show where the two marginal distributions differ. Braun calls the Q-Q plots an equipercentile equating function, or *eef*.

Consider, first, constructing a TAMP curve for just one population. If the size of the two samples from the population (the number of students from the population taking each test) is the same, then the Q-Q plot or TAMP curve is just a plot of the sorted scores from sample (test) 2 against the sorted scores from sample (test) 1. Even if the pairing of scores is known, the TAMP curve explicitly breaks the pairing and looks at only the marginal distributions. The TAMP methodology is best suited to situations in which the pairing is not known. In Braun's (1988) exposition, there is an implication that one need not plot all of these points, but only a systematic sample (say the 5th, 10th, . . . , 95th percentiles), and then connect the dots with a straight line. In the Immersion Report this implicit recommendation is made explicit and stronger, and all that is plotted is a solid TAMP curve, without any reference to the original data points. As noted below, the panel believes that it is much more informative to plot all the data points, connecting them with a line if desired, but preserving the location of the data. From this simple construction it is evident that the TAMP curve is a monotonic increasing function. If the two sample sizes are different, Braun suggests that the plot be created by calculating the quantiles of the empirical distribution function for some spread of percentiles.

In order to compare populations, a similar TAMP curve is computed for the other populations and the curves are then plotted on the same graph. The picture in Figure B-1 serves as an illustrative example, with TAMP curves for two populations, F and G, that have both taken an initial test, graded from 0 to 20, and a final test, which is also graded from 0 to 20. The solid curve shows that the proportion of students in the F population who scored less than 10 on the first test is the same as the proportion who scored less than 2 on the second test. One *cannot* conclude anything about an individual student's score from this graph.

The most important interpretation of the curves seems to be what Braun calls *uniformly retarded progress*. When one TAMP curve is always above the other, the population corresponding to the lower curve is said to show uniformly retarded progress with respect to the other population. This name comes about from the following observation. If one chooses a score on test 1 (say, 8, in Figure B-1),

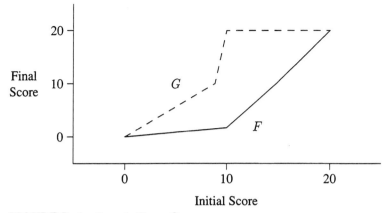

FIGURE B–1   Sample Tamp Curves

then for population F a student would have to score about 1.5 on the second test to retain the same rank in the class. A point on the curve represents a pair of scores, x and y, such that the observed frequency of scoring less than x on the first test is the same as the observed frequency of scoring less than y on the second test. For the same initial score of 8, a student from population G would need to score about 9, which is greater than 1.5, to retain his or her rank. This does not imply that every student in population G improves more than every student in population F. Quite the contrary! By subdividing the two populations on some other category (for example, gender or teacher), one may find that each of the subpopulations shows a reversal of the growth relationships.

To see how this can happen, consider a hypothetical data set that would give rise to the TAMP curve in Figure B–1. This example is adapted from Fienberg (1980). Suppose that there are 11,000 observations for students in population F and 10,100 observations for students in population G, with initial test score distribution given by:

Population	Initial Marginal Distributions (at time 0)	
	Between 0 and 9.99	Between 10 and 20
F_0	1,000/11,000	10,000/11,000
G_0	10,000/10,100	100/10,100

Note that this initial distribution is very unbalanced, with population F containing a high proportion of high scorers and population G containing a very high proportion of low scorers. Suppose that the final distribution is given by:

	Final Marginal Distributions (at time 1)	
Population	Between 0 and 9.99	Between 10 and 20
F_1	5,850/11,000	5,150/11,000
G_1	9,060/10,100	1,040/10,100

If the scores in each population are uniformly distributed in the range 0 to 9.99 and 10 to 20, then the initial and final distributions can be seen to correspond to the TAMP curve of Figure B–1. But the TAMP curve does not tell the entire story. In order to understand the progress of students in these two programs, one needs to know how many of the initial low/high scores in each population remained in the same category on the final test and how many changed categories. Suppose the transition table is given by:

	Final Score and Population			
Initial	Between 0 and 9.99		Between 10 and 20	
Score	F	G	F	G
0–9.99	$850/1,000$	$(9,000/10,000)$	$150/1.000$	$(1,000/10,000)$
10–20	$5,000/10,000$	$(60/100)$	$5,000/10,000$	$(40/100)$

This table says that 150 of the 1,000 people in population F who started out as low scorers became high scorers on the final test. The other 850 remained low scorers. Of the 10,000 initial high scorers in population F, 5,000 became low scorers and 5,000 remained high scorers. In population F, in contrast, 9,000 of 10,000 initial low scorers remained low scorers and 60 of 100 initial high scorers became low scorers. In other words, 15 percent of population F low scorers improved to the high scoring category on the final test while only 10 percent of population G low scorers showed a similar improvement. In fact, for every starting score, population F students raised their scores more than did population G students. Yet the TAMP curve for population F is uniformly below that for population G—a result that would appear to indicate uniformly retarded progress of population F.

This phenomenon, in which the apparent result of a TAMP curve analysis contradicts what is actually happening, is an instance of a phenomenon called Simpson's paradox. Simpson's paradox can occur in situations in which the distribution of initial test scores in the two populations is very different. It is one of many ways that the two populations might not be comparable.

If the TAMP curve is drawn as a solid line (as in the examples in the Immersion Study and Figure B–1), it is impossible to know that there is a difference in the

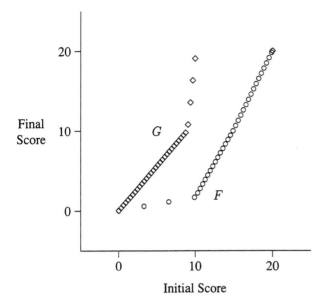

FIGURE B–2   Tamp Curves Illustrating Simpson's Paradox

initial test score distributions. If, instead, the TAMP curves actually plot the data points (or at least represent the local density of the data), unequal distributions will be readily apparent and should serve as a warning that Simpson's paradox may be a problem. Figure B–2 plots the same graphs with circles and diamonds representing data points (assuming uniform distributions and 34 people in each population). From these TAMP curves it is very easy to see that the two populations have very different marginal distributions. Nearly all students in population G score poorly on the first test, while most of those in population F score very well on the first test—exactly the situation that would warn of a difficulty in interpreting the TAMP analysis.

In summary, although TAMP provides a useful exploratory tool, users should be cautious about drawing strong conclusions. When the two populations are not comparable (for example, when the distribution of their initial tests scores are very unequal), interpreting differences in the TAMP curves is fraught with difficulties.

REFERENCES

Braun, H. I. (1988) A new approach to avoiding problems of scale in interpreting trends in mental measurement data. *Journal of Educational Measurement*, 25(3), 171–191.

Braun, H. I., and Holland, P. W. (1982) Observed-score test equating: A mathematical analysis of some ETS equating procedures. In P. W. Holland and D. B. Rubin, eds., *Test Equating*, pp. 9–49. New York: Academic Press.

Fienberg, S. E. (1980) *The Analysis of Cross-Classified Categorical Data* (second ed.). Cambridge, Mass.: MIT Press.

Gnanadesikan, R. (1977) *Methods for Statistical Data Analysis of Multivariate Data.* New York: Wiley.

Ramirez, D. J., Pasta, D. J., Yuen, S. D., Billings, D. K., and Ramey, D. R. (1991b) Final report: Longitudinal study of structured-english immersion strategy, early-exit and late-exit transitional bilingual education programs for language-minority children, Volume II. Technical report, Aquirre International, San Mateo, Calif.

Appendix C

Acronyms

Listed below are the acronyms used in this report:

AFDC	Aid to Families with Dependent Children
AIR	American Institutes for Research
ESEA	Elementary and Secondary Education Act
ESL	English as a Second Language
FEP	Fully English proficient
GAO	General Accounting Office
LEP	Limited English proficient
LM	Language-Minority
LM-LEP	language-minority limited-English-proficient
NCES	National Center for Education Statistics
NIE	National Institute of Education
OBE	Office of Bilingual Education
OCR	Office for Civil Rights
OPBE	Office of Planning, Budget, and Evaluation
OBEMLA	Office of Bilingual Education and Minority Language Affairs
Part C Committee	Education Division Coordinating Committee
RFPs	Requests for proposals
RTI	Research Triangle Institute
SAIP	Special Alternative Instructional Programs

Appendix D

Biographical Sketches of Panel Members and Staff

Stephen E. Fienberg *(Chair)* is professor of statistics and law and vice president (academic affairs) at York University, Toronto, Canada. He was formerly Maurice Falk professor of statistics and social science and dean of the College of Humanities and Social Sciences at Carnegie Mellon University, and he has held positions at the University of Chicago and the University of Minnesota. His principal research has been on the development of statistical methodology, especially in connection with the analysis of cross-classified data and, more recently, the design and analysis of experiments and sample surveys, as well as the application of statistics. He has been coordinating and applications editor of the *Journal of the American Statistical Association* and was cofounding editor of *Chance*. He was chair of the Committee on National Statistics from 1981 to 1987 and cochair of its Panel on Statistical Assessments as Evidence in the Courts. He received a B.Sc. honours degree in mathematics and statistics from the University of Toronto and A.M. and Ph.D. degrees in statistics from Harvard University.

Barbara F. Freed is professor of modern languages and chair of the modern languages program at Carnegie Mellon University. She was previously vice dean for language instruction at the University of Pennsylvania, where she was also director of the Regional Center for Language Proficiency. Her primary research interests include the integration of cognitive and social perspectives in second language acquisition, in both natural and classroom settings; she is also interested in the implications for instructional design and delivery that derive from these areas of inquiry. She received a B.A. degree in French from the University of Pennsylvania, an M.A. degree in Teaching English as a Second Language (TESOL) from Temple University, and a Ph.D. degree in linguistics in education from the University of Pennsylvania.

Kenji Hakuta is professor of education at Stanford University. His research areas are in language acquisition, bilingualism, and bilingual education. He has held teaching positions at Yale University and the University of California, Santa Cruz. He has been a fellow at the Center for Advanced Study in the Behavioral Sciences and a member of the Human Development and Aging Study Section of the National Institutes of Health, and he chairs the Board of Trustees of the Center for Applied Linguistics in Washington, D.C. He receiving Ph.D. degree in experimental psychology from Harvard University.

Lyle V. Jones is professor of psychology and director of the L. L. Thurstone Psychometric Laboratory at the University of North Carolina at Chapel Hill, where he previously served as vice chancellor and dean of the graduate school. He was a National Research Council postdoctoral fellow, a faculty member at the University of Chicago, and has held visiting faculty positions at the Universities of Illinois, Texas, and Washington. He is an elected member of the Institute of Medicine and an elected fellow of the American Academy of Arts and Sciences. At the National Research Council, he currently is a member of the Board on Associateship and Fellowship Programs and a member of the Report Review Committee. Among his recent publications are several that focus on historical trends in U.S. school achievement, with emphasis on trends for minority students. He attended Reed College, received B.S. and M.S. degrees from the University of Washington, and received a Ph.D. degree in psychology and statistics from Stanford University.

Kathryn Blackmond Laskey is associate professor in the Department of Systems Engineering at George Mason University. Her research interests include the use of probability models in artificial intelligence and methods of combining information from multiple sensors. Prior to joining the George Mason faculty, she was a principal scientist at Decision Science Consortium, where she developed computerized decision support systems and performed research in automated reasoning under uncertainty. She received a B.S. degree in mathematics from the University of Pittsburgh, an M.S. degree in mathematics from the University of Michigan, and a Ph.D. degree in statistics and public affairs from Carnegie Mellon University.

Michael M. Meyer *(Study Director)* is senior research scientist in the Departments of Statistics and Academic Computing and Media at Carnegie Mellon University. He previously held an academic appointment in the Department of Statistics at the University of Wisconsin–Madison. His research interests include statistical computing, categorical data analysis, and statistical modeling in neuropsychology. He has been the book reviews editor for *Chance* and is an associate editor for

Statistics and Computing. He received a B.A. honours degree in mathematics from the University of Western Australia and a Ph.D. degree in statistics from the University of Minnesota.

Luis C. Moll is associate professor in the Department of Language, Reading and Culture, College of Education, University of Arizona. He worked from 1979 to 1986 as research psychologist at the Laboratory of Comparative Human Cognition, University of California, San Diego. His research interests include childhood development and education, literacy learning and bilingualism, and sociocultural psychology. His recent publications include the analysis of the uses of knowledge in Latino households and the application of this knowledge in developing classroom practice. He was awarded a Ph.D. degree in early childhood development/educational psychology from the University of California, Los Angeles.

P. David Pearson is a professor in the area of literacy education in the Department of Curriculum and Instruction at the University of Illinois at Urbana-Champaign, where he also serves as dean of the College of Education. Prior to his appointment as dean, he served as codirector of the Center for the Study of Reading, where he continues to pursue a line of research in literacy instruction and assessment. He is originator and coeditor of two volumes of the *Handbook of Reading Research*, past editor of *Reading Research Quarterly*, and author of numerous research, policy, and practice articles about literacy processes, instruction, and assessment. He was the 1989 recipient of the Oscar Causey Award for contributions to research from the National Reading Conference and the 1990 William S. Gray Citation of Merit from the International Reading Association for his contributions to reading research and instruction. Professor Pearson received a bachelor's degree in history from the University of California at Berkeley and a Ph.D. degree from the University of Minnesota.

John E. Rolph is senior statistician at the RAND Corporation, where he has also served as head of RAND's statistical group. He has held faculty positions at University College London, Columbia University, the RAND Graduate School for Policy Studies, and the RAND/UCLA Health Policy Center. His research interests include empirical Bayes methods and the application of statistics to health policy, civil justice, criminal justice, and other policy areas. He has been an associate editor of two American Statistical Association journals and is currently a member of the National Research Council's Committee on National Statistics and Committee on Law and Justice. He received A.B. and Ph.D. degrees in statistics from the University of California, Berkeley.

Paul R. Rosenbaum is professor of statistics at the Wharton School of the University of Pennsylvania. Previously, he had been a senior research scientist at Educational Testing Service and taught at the University of Wisconsin–Madison. Much of his research has concerned the design and interpretation of observational studies. He received a B.A. degree in statistics from Hampshire College and M.A. and Ph.D. degrees in statistics from Harvard University.

Donald B. Rubin is professor of statistics and chair of the Department of Statistics at Harvard University. Previously, he was professor of statistics and of education at the University of Chicago and chair of the Statistics Research Group at Educational Testing Service. His research has dealt with causal inference in experimental and observational studies, missing data and nonresponse in surveys, and applied Bayesian statistics, including computational methods. He has been coordinating and applications editor of the *Journal of the American Statistical Association*; he is currently a member of the Committee on National Statistics. He received an A.B. degree from Princeton University and an M.S. degree in computer science and a Ph.D degree in statistics, both from Harvard University.

Keith F. Rust is associate director of the statistical group at Westat, Inc., in Rockville, Maryland. His former positions include supervisor in the Statistical Services Branch of the Australian Bureau of Statistics and visiting assistant professor at the Department of Biostatistics at the University of Michigan. His research interests include the methodology of the design and analysis of sample surveys. He is an editor of the *Journal of Official Statistics*. He received a B.A. honours degree in mathematics from the Flinders University of South Australia and M.S. and Ph.D. degrees in biostatistics from the University of Michigan.

Burton H. Singer is chair of the Department of Epidemiology and Public Health and Associate Dean for Public Health at Yale University. He is also chair of the Steering Committee for Social and Economic Research of the Tropical Disease Program at the World Health Organization, chair of the National Research Council's Committee on National Statistics, and a member of the board of directors of the Social Science Research Council. He has written books and articles on labor economics, epidemiology of tropical diseases, statistics, mathematical models in biology. He received a B.S. degree in engineering science and an M.S. degree in mechanical engineering from Case Institute of Technology and a Ph.D. degree in statistics from Stanford University.

Herbert L. Smith is associate professor of sociology and research associate in the Population Studies Center at the University of Pennsylvania. He taught previously at Indiana University and has been a visiting research fellow at the Population Sciences Division of the Rockefeller Foundation. He has written primarily on social demography, sociology of education, and research design. He received a B.A. degree in history and sociology from Yale University and M.A. and Ph.D. degrees in sociology in population and human ecology from the University of Michigan.

References

Atkinson, R., and Jackson, G., eds. (1992) *Research and Education Reform: Roles for the Office of Educational Research and Improvement.* Committee on the Federal Role in Education Research, Commission on Behavioral and Social Sciences and Education, National Research Council. Washington, D.C.: National Academy Press.

Baker, K. A., and de Kanter, A. A., eds. (1983) *Bilingual Education: A Reappraisal of Federal Policy.* Lexington, Mass.: Lexington Books.

Box, G. E. P., and Draper, N. R. (1969) *Evolutionary Operation: A Statistical Method for Process Improvement.* New York: John Wiley.

Box, G. E. P., and Draper, N. R. (1987) *Empirical Model-building and Response Surfaces.* New York: John Wiley.

Braun, H. I. (1988) A new approach to avoiding problems of scale in interpreting trends in mental measurement data. *Journal of Educational Measurement,* 25(3), 171–191.

Braun, H. I., and Holland, P. W. (1982) Observed-score test equating: A mathematical analysis of some ETS equating procedures. In P. W. Holland and D. B. Rubin, eds., *Test Equating,* pp. 9–49. New York: Academic Press.

Burkheimer, Jr., G. J., Conger, A. J., Dunteman, G. H., Elliott, B. G., and Mowbray, K. A. (1989) Effectiveness of services for language-minority limited-english-proficient students (2 vols). Technical report, Research Triangle Institute, Research Triangle Park, N.C.

Campbell, D. (1969) Prospective: Artifact and control. In R. Rosenthal and R. Rosnow, eds., *Artifact in Behavioral Research.* New York: Academic Press.

Campbell, D. T. (1978) Experiemental design: Quasi-experimental design. In W. H. Kruskal and J. M. Tanur, eds., *International Encyclopedia of Statistics,* pp. 299–304. New York: The Free Press.

Chambers, J. M., Cleveland, W. S., Kleiner, B., and Tukey, P. A. (1983) *Graphical Methods for Data Analysis.* Belmont, Calif.: Wadsworth International Group.

Cochran, W. G. (1965) The planning of observational studies of human populations (with discussion). *Journal of the Royal Statistical Society, Series A,* 128, 124–135.

Cochran, W. G. (1977) *Sampling Techniques* (third ed.). New York: John Wiley.

Cook, T. D., and Campbell, D. T. (1979) *Quasi-experimentation*. Chicago, Ill.:   Rand McNally.

Cornfield, J., Haenszel, W., Hammond, E., and others (1959) Smoking and lung cancer: Recent evidence and a discussion of some questions. *Journal of the National Cancer Institute*, 22, 173–203.

Cox, D. R. (1958a) The interpretation of the effects of non-additivity in the latin square. *Biometrika*, 45, 69–73.

Cox, D. R. (1958b) *The Planning of Experiments*. New York: John Wiley.

Crawford, J. (1989) *Bilingual Education: History, Politics, Theory, and Practice*. Trenton, N.J.:   Crane Publishing Co.

Dannoff, M. N. (1978) Evaluation of the impact of ESEA Title VII Spanish/English bilingual education programs. Technical report, American Institutes for Research, Washington, D.C.

Development Associates (1984a) The descriptive phase report of the national longitudinal study of the effectiveness of services for LMLEP students. Technical report, Development Associates Inc., Arlington, Va.

Development Associates (1984b) Overview of the research design plans for the national longitudinal study study of the effectiveness of services for LMLEP students, with appendices. Technical report, Development Associates Inc., Arlington, Va.

Development Associates (1986) Year 1 report of the longitudinal phase. Technical report, Development Associates Inc., Arlington, Va.

DuMouchel, W. H., and Harris, J. E. (1983) Bayes methods for combining the results of cancer studies in humans and other species (with discussion). *Journal of the American Statistical Association*, 78, 293–308.

Duncan, O. D. (1975) *Introduction to Structural Equation Models*. New York: Academic Press.

Ellickson, P. L., and Bell, R. M. (1992) Challenges to social experiments: A drug prevention example. *Journal of Research in Crime and Delinquency*, 29, 79–101.

Evans, A. S. (1976) Causation and disease: The Henle-Kock postulates revisited. *Yale Journal of Biology and Medicine*, 49, 175–195.

Fienberg, S. E. (1980) *The Analysis of Cross-Classified Categorical Data* (second ed.). Cambridge, Mass.:   MIT Press.

Fienberg, S. E., Singer, B., and Tanur, J. (1985) Large-scale social experimentation in the united states. In A. C. Atkinson and S. E. Fienberg, eds., *A Celebration of Statistics: The ISI Centenary Volume*, pp. 287–326. New York: Springer Verlag.

Fisher, R. A. (1925) *Statistical Methods for Research Workers* (first ed.). Edinburgh: Oliver and Boyd.

Fishman, J. A. (1977) The social science perspective. In *Bilingual Education: Current Perspectives. Vol. 1: Social Science*, pp. 1–49. Rosslyn, Va.:   Center for Applied Linguistics.

Freedman, R., and Takeshita, J. (1969) *Family Planning in Taiwan: An Experiment in Social Change*. Princeton, N.J.:   Princeton University Press.

Gnanadesikan, R. (1977) *Methods for Statistical Data Analysis of Multivariate Data*. New York: Wiley.

Groves, R. M. (1989) *Survey Errors and Survey Costs*. New York: John Wiley.

Hakuta, K. (1986) *Mirror of Language: The Debate on Bilingualism*. New York: Basic Books.

Hoaglin, D. C., Light, R., McPeek, B., Mosteller, F., and Stoto, M. (1982) *Data for Decisions*. Cambridge, Mass.:   Abt Associates.

Johnson, N. L., and Kotz, S., eds. (1982–1989) *The Encyclopedia of Statistical Sciences* (10 volumes). New York: John Wiley.

Kasprzyk, D., Duncan, G., Kalton, G., and Singh, M. P. (1987) *Panel Surveys.* New York: John Wiley.

Kempthorne, O. (1952) *The Design and Analysis of Experiments.* New York: John Wiley.

Kish, L. (1965) *Survey Sampling.* New York: John Wiley.

Kruskal, W. H., and Mosteller, F. (1988) Representative sampling. In S. Kotz and N. L. Johnson, eds., *Encyclopedia of Statistical Sciences*, volume 8, pp. 77–81. New York: John Wiley and Sons.

Kruskal, W. H., and Tanur, J. M., eds. (1978) *The International Encyclopedia of Statistics* (2 volumes). New York: Macmillan and the Free Press.

Lambert, W. E. (1980) Two faces of bilingualism. In *Focus, No. 3.* Rosslyn, Va.: National Clearinghouse for Bilingual Education.

Lambert, W. E. (1992) Pros, cons, and limits to quantitative approaches in foreign language research. In B. F. Freed, ed., *Foreign Language Acquisition Research and the Classroom*, chapter 19, pp. 321–337. Lexington, Mass.: D. C. Heath and Co.

Little, R. J. A., and Rubin, D. B. (1987) *Statistical Analysis with Missing Data.* New York: John Wiley.

Madow, W. G., Nisselson, J., and Olkin, I., eds. (1983) *Incomplete Data in Sample Surveys, Volume 1: Report and Case Studies.* Panel on Incomplete Data, Committee on National Statistics, Commission on Behavioral and Social Sciences and Education, National Research Council. New York: Academic Press.

Marini, M. M., and Singer, B. (1988) Causality in the social sciences. In C. C. Clogg, ed., *Sociological Methodology 1988*, chapter 11, pp. 347–409. Washington, D.C.: American Sociological Association.

Marquis, W. G., Newhouse, J. P., Duan, N., Keeler, E. B., Leibowitz, A., and Marqui, M. S. (1987) Health insurance and the demand for medical care: Evidence from a randomized experiment. *American Economic Review*, 77, 252–277.

Mason, W. M., Wong, G. Y., and Entwisle, B. (1984) Contextual analysis through the multilevel linear model. In S. Leinhardt, ed., *Sociological Methodology 1984*, pp. 72–103. Washington, D.C.: American Sociological Association.

Miller, R. G. (1981) *Simultaneous Statistical Inference* (second ed.). New York: Springer Verlag.

Mosteller, F., Fienberg, S. E., and Rourke, R. E. K. (1983) *Beginning Statistics with Data Analysis.* Reading, Mass.: Addison-Wesley.

Mosteller, F., and Tukey, J. W. (1982) Combination of results of stated precision: I. the optimistic case. *Utilitas Mathematica*, 21, 155–178.

Mosteller, F., and Tukey, J. W. (1984) combination of results of stated precision: II. a more realistic case. In P. S. R. S. Rao and J. Sedransk, eds., *W. G. Cochran's Impact on Statistics*, pp. 223–252. New York: John Wiley.

National Clearinghouse for Bilingual Education Forum (1982) Update: Part C bilingual education research. National Clearinghouse for Bilingual Education, Rosslyn, Va.

National Research Council (1981) *New Directions in the Rehabilitation of Criminal Offenders.* Panel on Research on Rehabilitative Techniques, Committee on Research on Law Enforcement and the Administration of Justice, Commission on Behavioral and Social Sciences and Education, National Research Council. Washington, D.C.: National Academy Press.

Neyman, J. (1923) On the application of probability theory to agricultural experiments. *Roczniki Nauk Rolniczvch*, X, 1–51. English translation: *Statistical Science* , 1990, 5, 465–480.

Ramirez, D. J., Yuen, S. D., Ramey, D. R., and Pasta, D. J. (1991a) Final report: Longitudinal study of structured-english immersion strategy, early-exit and late-exit transitional bilingual education programs for language-minority children, Volume I. Technical report, Aquirre International, San Mateo, Calif.

Ramirez, D. J., Pasta, D. J., Yuen, S. D., Billings, D. K., and Ramey, D. R. (1991b) Final report: Longitudinal study of structured-english immersion strategy, early-exit and late-exit transitional bilingual education programs for language-minority children, Volume II. Technical report, Aquirre International, San Mateo, Calif.

Rosenbaum, P., and Kreiger, A. (1990) Sensitivity of two-sample permutation inferences in observational studies. *Journal of the American Statistical Association*, 85, 493–498.

Rosenbaum, P. R. (1984) The consequences of adjustment for a concomitant variable that has been affected by the treatment. *Journal of the Royal Statistical Society Series A*, 147, 656–666.

Rosenbaum, P. R. (1986) Dropping out of high school in the United States: An observational study. *Journal of Educational Statistics*, 11, 207–224.

Rosenbaum, P. R. (1987) The role of a second control group in an observational study (with discussion). *Statistical Science*, 2, 292–316.

Rosenbaum, P. R. (1991) Discussing hidden bias in observational studies. *Annals of Internal Medicine*, 115(11), 901–905.

Rosenbaum, P. R., and Rubin, D. B. (1983) Assessing sensitivity to an unobserved binary covariate in an observational study with binary outcome. *Journal of the Royal Statistical Society, Series B*, 45, 212–218.

Rubin, D. B. (1974) Estimating the causal effects of treatments in randomized and nonrandomized studies. *Journal of Educational Psychology*, 66, 688–701.

Rubin, D. B. (1978) Bayesian inference for causal effects: The role of randomization. *Annals of Statistics*, 6, 34–58.

Rubin, D. B. (1984) William G. Cochran's contributions to the design, analysis, and evaluation of observational studies. In P. S. R. S. Rao and J. Sedransk, eds., *W. G. Cochran's Impact on Statistics*, pp. 37–69. New York: Wiley.

Samaniego, F. J., and Eubank, L. A. (1991) A statistical analysis of California's case study project in bilingual education. Technical Report 208, Division of Statistics, University of California, Davis.

Skinner, C. J., Holt, D., and Smith, T. M. F. (1989) *Analysis of Complex Surveys*. New York: John Wiley.

Spencer, B. D., and Foran, W. (1991) Sampling probabilities for aggregations, with applications to NELS:88 and other educational longitudinal surveys. *Journal of Educational Statistics*, 16(1), 21–34.

Swain, M. (1992) French immersion and its offshoots: Getting two for one. In B. F. Freed, ed., *Foreign Language Acquisition Research and the Classroom*, chapter 19, pp. 321–337. Lexington, Mass.: D. C. Heath and Co.

Tharp, R., and Gallimore, R. (1979) The ecology of program research and evaluation: A model of succession evaluation. In L. Sechrest, M. Philips, R. Redner, and S. West, eds., *Evaluation Studies Review Annual: 4*. Beverly Hills, Calif.: Sage Publications.

U.S. Department of Education (1991) *The Condition of Bilingual Education in the Nation: A Report to the Congress and the President*. Office of the Secretary. Washington, D.C.: U.S. Department of Education.

U.S. General Accounting Office (1987) Bilingual education: A new look at the research evidence. Briefing Report to the Chairman, Committee on Education, Labor, House of Representatives, GAO/PEMD-87-12BR.

Wachter, K. W., and Straf, M. L., eds. (1990) *The Future of Meta-Analysis*. Committee on National Statistics, Commission on Behavioral and Social Sciences and Education, National Research Council. New York: Russell Sage Foundation.

Welch, B. L. (1937) On the z-test in randomized blocks and latin squares. *Biometrika*, 29, 21–52.

Wilk, M. B. (1955) The randomization analysis of a generalized randomized block design. *Biometrika*, 42, 70–79.

Willig, A. (1987) Meta-analysis of selected studies in the effectiveness of bilingual education. *Review of Educational Research*, 57(3), 351–362.

Yates, F. (1981) *Sampling Methods for Censuses and Surveys* (fourth ed.).   New York: Macmillan.

Yates, F., and Cochran, W. G. (1938) The analysis of groups of experiments. *The Journal of Agricultural Science*, XXVIII(IV), 556–580.

Yin, R. K. (1989) *Case-Study Research. Design and Methods* (revised ed.). Newbury Park, Calif.:   Sage Publications.